THE TOUGHEST DAYS OF GRIEF

Making It Through

THE
TOUGHEST
DAYS OF
GRIEF

MEG WOODSON

Zondervan Publishing House
Grand Rapids, Michigan

A Division of HarperCollins*Publishers*

The Toughest Days of Grief
Copyright © 1994 by Meg Woodson

Requests for information should be addressed to:
Zondervan Publishing House
Grand Rapids, MI 49530

Library of Congress Cataloging-in-Publication Data

Woodson, Meg.
    The toughest days of grief / Meg Woodson.
        p.   cm.
    ISBN 0-310-40001-5 (pbk.)
    1. Grief—Religious aspects—Christianity. 2. Consolation.
3. Woodson, Meg.
I. Title
BV4905.2W656   1994
248.8'6—dc20
                                                                93-6743
                                                                    CIP
                                                                     AC

The names and at times the identities of the grievers in this book have been
changed.

Edited by Judith Markham, Blue Water Ink
Cover design by Sarah Slattery
Cover photo by D. Jeanene Tiner Photographs, House Springs, MO 63051

94 95 96 97 98 99 / ❖ DH / 10 9 8 7 6 5 4 2 1

Dedication

· ·

*To
Charlene Hanford,
who
grieved with us
and now
for whom we grieve*

*And to
Father Joseph Zubricky,
who
blessed me
when
I mourned*

· · · · · · · · · · · · · · ·

*With thanks to Judith Markham of Blue Water
Ink, Grand Rapids, who worked with her soft
heart and her skilled editorial mind—and with
incredible patience—to save me from myself at
many points in this book.*

Contents

CHAPTER 1

The Special Pain of Special Occasions

> It doesn't matter so much what you do to get through these days, just that you do something, and that you plan ahead of time what you will do—a month ahead when your hands get clammy and your heart begins its wild beat.
>
> Mwalimu Imara

*N*othing hurts like the loss of someone you love. The pain is raw and strange and it frightens you, even if you've known loss before, and the pain keeps on till you can't bear it, and you can't make it go away.

All days are bad when you're grieving, but some days are worse than others: your wedding anniversary, Memorial Day, Thanksgiving, Easter. How do you make it through these days?

I don't want any of these days to be.

"Everyone wants to help me celebrate my birthday," Sue, a bereaved mother, sobs in my office, "but Suzette drew me pictures on my birthday—every year. I don't want to know when it's my birthday. Or Halloween. Or Christmas. I don't want any of these days to be."

I learned about the special pain of special occasions when my son, Joey, died. Joey came and went in twelve quicksilver years and never asked for much, only that I know what he was doing and tell him how good he was at doing it, and that I love him, and he didn't have to ask for that.

I knew that God would not let Joey die because I knew God knew I could not live without one person in my life who was satisfied with me.

I lost my innocence when my son, Joseph Woodson, Jr., died of cystic fibrosis,* and I no longer believed that C. F. would not kill my daughter, Peggie, too, my only other child. Peggie was my judge. Peggie looked like me, hurt in the same super-sensitive way I hurt, was lonely a lot. Peggie was my prickly flesh-of-my-flesh friend, and I was less lonely for the twenty-three years I had her than I ever imagined I could be.

I lost my immortality when Margaret Ann Woodson, my namesake, my nemesis, died, and I wanted to die, too. Especially on my children's birthdays and death days and

---

* A disease that affects the digestive and respiratory systems.

on Mother's Day—barren days on which I ached to be *with child–with child* again.

This book does not grow just out of my personal experience, however, or out of my professional training as the grief counselor I have become, but also out of the experiences of friends and clients who have shared their grief with me.

Jan, for example, who lost her four-month-old son through death and, eight years later, in her thirties, her husband through divorce. "When I lost my child, I lost my child," she says. "When I lost Craig, I lost myself. Couldn't love myself, couldn't trust myself. I sobbed day and night."

And Grace, widowed and in failing health in her sixties. "My mother died when I was fifteen. My father worked nights, and I got shifted around. For a while I slept down the street with a friend. In the morning I walked back up the street in my pajamas and robe. When I married Al, I finally had someone who cared about what happened to me for some reason besides that I was a responsibility. Now . . . I feel like I'm walking up the street in my pajamas and robe again."

And Ted, twenty-four, grieving for the childhood he never had. And Jim, who became a widower in his seventies, never so much as having bought a loaf of bread. And John, who lost both his parents. "I'm an orphan," he cries, "a forty-six-year-old orphan."

And Sue, whom you've already met.

The special days are days of traditions, traditions of love.

The special pain these people—and you—feel on special days is an intensification of the pain you feel every day.

Of course you feel the absence of your loved one—your *love*—more on the days when he or she was always present, more present than on other days. Of course you feel the emptiest on the days when you once felt the most filled with love.

The special days are days of tradition, traditions of love, and now these best of traditions have been broken—in the worst of ways.

You're exhausted. Your attention span has shrunk. You wonder if you've lost your memory altogether. You haven't. These conditions will lift as the heaviest of your grief lifts, but I honor the way you are right now by inserting headings into this book—pauses—in which you can pause if you desire, to rest, to reflect.

I don't want to take away the pain of your special occasions, not yet. I couldn't if I wanted to. I don't want to take all their pain away ever, but perhaps I can suggest ways to help you ease their pain.

1. Plan ahead. Build structure—support—into these days. It's being caught off-guard that does you in.

2. Take care of yourself on these days. Rest. Treat yourself.

3. Feel the grief triggered by these days. Feel a little of the grief away.

4. Let people hold you on these days.

5. Let God hold your heart in His hands on these days.

6. Remember—honor—*hold*—your *love* in special ways on these days.

Perhaps I can light a candle to shine alongside the blackest days of your grief to help you see your way through them—and beyond.

CHAPTER 2

Your First Vacation

And then my heart with pleasure fills,
And dances with the daffodils.
> William Wordsworth

And if you have given sorrow the space its gentle origins demand, then you may truly say: life is beautiful and rich. So beautiful and so rich that it makes you want to believe in God. . . . Give your sorrow all the space and shelter in yourself that is its due. . . .
> Ellie Hillesum

*W*hat? Thoughts of vacation? So early in the book?

Yes. In part because I suspect that vacations may be the hardest of the special days for you, that feelings of pleasure may be harder for you to handle than feelings of pain. And in part because the feelings of pleasure dealt with in this chapter apply to all your special days.

How disrespectful to your *love*, you think, even to consider having a good time.

But to the contrary, how respectful to your *love* that you must lighten your despair over your loss or be lost yourself.

Take advantage of a vacation's near-mystic healing powers.

Take care, my fellow-griever. Rest. Rest some more. Be patient with yourself. Treat yourself in special ways on all your special days.

And, especially, treat yourself to a vacation. Yes, I know that thinking about a vacation turns your stomach queasy with guilt, and with dread of the empty place beside you on the blanket at the beach, or of the hand that will not hold yours as you climb the steep path.

You may not have spent the time you wanted to spend with mother or brother or friend during the working year, but when you went away on vacation together, your heart feasted on them till you were *full up*.

And what about coming home? If you go away, you have to come home—to an empty house.

Every year Joe, my husband, and I go to a place affectionately called *Camp*, though it is not a camp, for part of our vacation. Our daughter, Peg, only went to Camp with us once, ten years ago, yet every year as we nestle into Camp's quiet pine woods, I miss her with a disquiet I don't feel the rest of the year. Why?

Well, Camp *sees to it* that we have the time and inner quiet in which to remember her, not on vacation with us, just *with us*.

Yes, vacations are hard on us grievers; yet it's almost never too soon to think about taking one.

I say it's *almost* never too soon to think about a vacation because there is the early stage of grief experts call *shock* or *numbness*. I think of it as the *bashed-in* stage, though I don't stress stages. Loss has dealt you a knock-down blow. *Where am I?* you cry. *Who am I?* No, your face isn't swollen purple, but it feels, and looks, *bashed-in*.

Time will bring you through this period. Discolorations of the spirit fade whether you want them to or not. But time needs help with deeper healing.

Not that you use a vacation to run away from your grief. Only grieving will relieve your grief; only feeling your pain will lessen your feeling of it. But right now you may be so weighed down with your grief that you can't feel anything.

Perhaps a grief counselor has prescribed an antidepressant to lift you up enough so that you can feel again—grief and joy. I'm for antidepressants when they're needed. All kinds. And I see vacations as one of the best.

Yes, I know that you may have lost the person who would ordinarily put an arm around you on the couch and plan a vacation with you. I'm sorry about that, and if you need to cry, go ahead, weep—weep, all by yourself there.

But when you've wept yourself out this time around, dry your eyes and create a joy-to-come for yourself. We'll talk later in the chapter about *expectations* other than vacations you can plan, but don't give up on a vacation unless you must.

Take advantage of a vacation's near-mystic healing powers.

The widest cracks in our pain opened on the beach, cracks wide enough to let the moisture-laden ocean light shine through.

"Come take a peek at these brochures on Caribbean cruises," Joe said to me in the early days after Peggie's death.

"I can't make decisions right now, Joe." I jerked away when he tried to pull me down beside him. "How can you talk about cruises at a time like this?"

But Joe persisted, day by day, encouraging me to *take a peek* out of my world of pain into a world of less pain. "How about the Mountain Top Inn in Vermont? Or would the ocean be better for you?"

Three months after Peggie died, we settled into a rambling old inn, complete with mermaid banister posts, on the tip of Cape Cod.

"Remember when Peggie and Joey were little, Meg, how they explored any place we stayed the minute we checked in and then dragged us out to show us where everything was?"

We feasted in the inn's Yellow Room overlooking the sea. "Yellow is—I mean, yellow *was* Peggie's favorite color, Joe."

We nested in a sheltered place overlooking the harbor. We read there. We cried for Peggie there. And sometimes we didn't cry for Peggie there.

"Have you noticed, Joe, that vacation grief is more restoring than at-home grief?"

We visited a lighthouse. We whale-watched. We had a good enough time that we could feel our bad time in the depths in which we needed to feel it and not be destroyed by it.

The widest cracks in our pain opened as we splashed along the edge of the icy water, cracks wide enough to let the moisture-laden ocean light shine through.

The incident I remember best took place on the first day of that first vacation. We headed for the ocean early on, even though a northeaster was blowing the beach into a wild, abandoned place. The cold gusted through us.

We set up our lawn chairs in the shelter of a sand dune, snuggled together under a blanket, and listened to the ocean roar.

Then Joe brought our tape recorder from the car with his favorite tape, Handel's *Messiah*. He turned the music up so we could hear the Hallelujah Chorus over the crashing of the surf, but the sounds merged inside us into one.

And I thought about our other trip to the Cape, twenty-four years earlier. Our marriage was four years old, but we had no children. We'd tried, we'd prayed—but no children.

Then came our first Cape Cod vacation, in our miniature travel trailer, and one pure morning when I was floating on the mild swells of the bay and felt a touch of nausea. "I'm pregnant," I'd gasped—and was.

So, I mused, as I pressed leeward into the giant sand dune, *the last time we were here Peg was on her way to us, and this time Peg has gone away from us.*

Even now I do not want to admit to the completeness of it.

I don't know why I thought of the pregnancy incident then. I don't remember thinking of it when we decided on the Cape for our vacation. Perhaps the blending of the other-world music with the music of this world convinced me that I was supposed to be on that spot—that God was cheering us on, on the first day of our first vacation after Peggie *went away*.

Difficulties loom in the blackness as impossibilities.

We worried about spending savings on our Cape Cod vacation. There is, however, a time to worry and a time to splurge, and a time to grieve is a time to be good to yourself, and to let others be good to you, too.

Jan's finances were limited after her divorce, so she took trips with friends going to business conventions, stayed in their rooms, and didn't eat much.

The smell of hopelessness and helplessness pervades the bog of our grief. Difficulties loom in the darkness as impossibilities. Taking initiative comes hard; being sucked into thick, clinging depression doesn't take initiative.

"You have to force yourself," says Jan, "to take some first little step on your own. I took four vacations in the first four years after my divorce, and every vacation was a way of getting on with my life. Learning that I could manage the details Craig and I had once managed together gave me a wonderful sense of satisfaction."

After our son, Joey, died, my sister in California said, "I'll fly in for the funeral if you like, but if you'd rather, I'll fly you out here later on." Joe and Peggie and I flew *out there*.

I still remember walking into a souvenir shop looking for something to bring back to—I still remember the sudden stop, the sick lurch in my stomach. I still remember walking into the next souvenir shop . . . and the next . . .

I still remember coming home to a tomblike house, waiting for Joey to plunge down the stairs yelling, "Mama, Mama, you're home."

Yet the concentrated time Joe and Peg and I spent on our once-in-a-lifetime trip to sunny California helped mold us into a family of three, a family that *aaaahed* together over the Grand Canyon, and *eeeehed* together in Disneyland's Pirate's Cove, a family that cried together but a family that laughed together, too. And with an aunt and uncle and niece, a larger family that enlarged our sense of mooring at a time when we had drifted loose from harbor.

And a larger family needn't be made up of blood relations. At home Jan couldn't avoid people who took Craig's side in their divorce. Vacations got her away with people who supported her.

Try not to cry too much, Mother.

"Isn't it too soon for you to be taking a vacation?" a friend asked after Joey's death.

Well, it was soon even for one who believes it's almost never too soon. Plan your good times ahead of time when you can; looking forward to something special is almost as therapeutic as the special thing itself. We wished we could have waited to go on our California trip, but it was almost time for school to start for Peg, so we did not wait, and we suspected that more than one person whispered about that behind our backs.

Wearing black when you're in mourning is out of fashion, but believing that enjoying yourself makes a statement on how little you miss your *unloved one* is not.

But would the person you've lost want you to shut yourself up in your house? Ask yourself: Was his concern when he was dying that you'd have too easy a time?

"Try not to cry too much, Mother," Peggie said in anticipation of her death. "I mean, I'm not saying don't cry at all. That's dumb. But don't cry too much."

One of the conventions Jan went to was in Orlando, and she enjoyed herself—unbelievable—without Craig, in some ways, more than she would have enjoyed herself with him.

"When Craig got lost, he drove around in circles rather than ask for help; now I stopped for directions. When I went away with Craig, I always did what he wanted to do; now I got up at 6:30 in the morning and sat by the pool if I wanted to. I had no choice but to do it without Craig, but I could choose to do it. It was bittersweet.

"On vacation it came to me in bits and pieces—this being single isn't all bad."

I tell you, my fellow-griever, all these years after my children's deaths, I still feel mortally wounded at times. I still feel sad. But I also feel strong. I feel peaceful. I feel hopeful. I feel loved. I feel alive in a way I never knew I could. I *feel* in a way I never did—and vacations have played a significant part in this transformation.

We ought not to deny our grief, but we ought not to deny everything but our grief either.

I feel close to Gary, my son, with a boa around my neck.

I once sat next to a woman in a grief group whose son had died in a mountain-climbing accident. He'd kept a boa constrictor as a pet at home, she said. He liked to hang it around his neck. Liked to hang it around his mother's neck.

"After Gary died," his mother said, "I was at a nature museum, and a man asked for a volunteer to come up front and hang a boa around their neck.

" 'I'm going up,' I told my friends.

" 'You can't do a crazy thing like that,' they said.

"But I went up anyway. I feel close to Gary, my son, with a boa around my neck."

Then she told us that her son had also taught her to rumba. "Every time I hear a rumba," she said in a voice that dared anyone to object, "I rumba. I don't care where I am. I feel close to Gary, my son, when I'm doing the rumba."

She handed me a picture of herself wearing . . . a stole. I'd never seen a stole that reached almost to the ground—aghhhh, the snake.

My stomach somersaulted as I passed the picture to the person next to me. That snake would not have comforted me.

So? Was I Gary's mother?

Do whatever comforts, whatever strengthens *you*. Do the rumba with a boa constrictor around your neck—unless the boa constrictor objects.

But whether you go away on vacation or schedule get-away pleasures into your stay-at-home week, into every day of your grief, aim at keeping: in touch with nature; out of touch with *the scene of the crime*; and in touch with people.

Looking up at a skyscraper won't make a survivor out of you, but looking up at a mountain will help.

One day in the early months after Joey died, Joe coaxed me out of my bed, onto my bicycle, and into the tree-lined grounds of our local community college. All these years later I remember how we skimmed along with the sun braising our cheeks and the wind billowing our shirts and how I thought, *I want to feel alive again.*

And all these years later I remember an evening in the early months after Peggie died when I took a solitary walk through our neighborhood, an evening so clear and cool I wanted to open my mouth and gulp the freshness in. And I thought, *I feel alive again.*

Nature at its best will do that for you. Because the more sunlight that enters your eyes the less prone you are to depression? Possibly. Because the more you exercise the more endorphins enter your bloodstream and the less prone you are to depression? Probably. Because your nature reflects nature's mood? Yes, surely.

Emotional strain exhausts you. If your loss comes unexpectedly, shock drains the energy from your body. If your loss comes slowly, drawn-out dread does the same, to say nothing of anger.

Nature rests you.

Look up at a mountain when the sun is high and you feel as tall and strong as the mountain. The gales of your grief still blow, but they don't flatten you as they once did. Looking up at a skyscraper won't make a survivor out of you, but looking up at a mountain will help.

It has to do with beauty, a quality attributed by Webster to "whatever pleases or satisfies . . . as by line, color, form, texture, proportion, rhythmic motion. . . ." In pleasing us in so many ways, nature soothes our displeasure. And, oh, how displeasured we grievers are.

I visited an art museum after Joey died and found myself sitting in front of one painting, *Blue Boy*, taking it in and taking it in and feeling not-so-empty within. Only now does the significance of the painting being of a boy occur to me. How unlike my lost boy that ruffled, patrician Blue

Boy was; yet how he fed my hungry heart with a boy's beauty.

Trust your instincts. You know what you need.

You know that you need to delight yourself with artistic representations of the beauty of nature, of life—paintings, music, literature.

But even more, you know that you need to absorb nature itself.

Only standing at the ocean's edge do you *hear* the sea gull's call, *feel* the damp sand beneath your feet, *taste* the brine on your lips, *smell* the tide, *see* the rippling, glistening unendingness of it all.

Perhaps, though, underlying other reasons, nature heals you when you're grieving because it approximates Ultimate Beauty—God.

You may feel only anger at God right now. "God is not the creator of beauty but of ugliness," you cry, "of decay." I've felt that way, too.

But I do not believe it was an accident on the first day of our vacation after Peggie *went away* that Handel's music throbbed in accord with the ocean's large lament. When God, the Creator, cannot speak with us directly, He speaks through His creation, whether we want Him to or not. Whether we believe in Him at all.

I like to think that as the ocean choked out its wild sobs that day, God, too, sobbed in frenzy with His two grieving children bent double on their green-and-white striped K-Mart lawn chairs. Nature at its worst will heal you, too.

So why don't I drive forty minutes to feel Lake Erie's fair breezes on my cheeks? Why don't you walk five minutes to greet a maple tree in feisty red? Why don't we grievers pause in our own backyards to smell the sweet sweet-peas along our grieving ways?

Please, you owe this to yourself.

Oh, to be pampered, diverted from the incapacitating impact of where it happened.

And remove yourself, please, from the hardness and humdrumness of everyday life. Keep out of touch with *the scene of the crime.*

"Every minute things were difficult," Jan says of her time at home after her divorce. "I had to restructure my life. Everything had to be done *now*. On vacation I had no responsibility except *to be*. When I was in a new place with no associations with the past, I began to believe I could have a new life."

Grief work is the most exhausting work in the world. All is lost, we cry, you and I. Oh, to be pampered, enchanted—diverted from the incapacitating impact of where it happened, that it happened.

A few months before Joey died, I found myself longing to redecorate our living room. My husband is a minister, and we've always lived in parsonages not decorated to our tastes. How I longed to make one room in one parsonage my creation.

Of course it won't happen, I told myself, because I'd have to have Early American carpeting and wallpaper, and the church can't afford carpeting, and I can't ask for wallpaper when paint is cheaper.

But, then, though I'd told no one of my dream, the chairman of our church board came up to me one day and apropos of nothing said, "Go pick out any carpet you want for your living room, Meg," and he canvassed the congregation to pay for it.

Then, after the red and blue braided carpeting had been installed, a new member of the board took charge of the parsonage, a man who had such a love affair going with wallpaper that he *could not paint*. "Pick out any wallpaper you want for your living room," he told me, and later someone else told me he paid for the colonial-blue wallpaper himself.

And, then, after Joey died—ah, desolation—I spent weeks, months, roaming the depths of The Red Brick Store and The Village Square Shoppe hunting down hand-dipped candles ... a painting of Williamsburg Church framed in walnut. I *got away* into a two-hundred-year-old time, into a secure and simple place.

To this day visitors enter the living room I created during that time and say, "I feel love in this room."

How well God knew me, helping me create therapeutic pleasure for myself that was as much my own as my pain.

So there it is, and all within an hour and a half from home.

"I go garage sale-ing every Thursday," says Gracie. "I get outside, I get exercise gettin' in and out of the car and walkin' to the houses, and I meet all kinds of crazy people. Thursday is my bummin' day.

"And once a month, I keep my grandson, Marky, over-night. We go to the toy store. We sing in the car at the top of our lungs, 'You are my sunshine.'

"Then, too, when the spirit moves me, I call this friend who's retired and we drive down to Amish country. It's only an hour and a half away, but you see old women holding the reins in Amish buggies. Al and I used to go to an Amish village called Charm and watch the girls in the schoolyard in their dark dresses and white caps. Al would say we'd been to Charm School.

"I also have my reading days. I drop everything when I find a Harlequin Romance in a garage sale. I read in a recliner in my living room, but I call my reading days the days *I run away from home.*"

Gracie also tells me about her spider plant in a hanging basket and her coleus, eighteen inches high on three stalks. "I nurse my plants along. They bring nature inside the house and inside me. I feel bad when they die, but if I can save one little piece and root it, I have the feeling that life goes on."

So there it is, and all within an hour and a half of home—nature and getting away and people, though not all three in every activity.

Being alone in a motel room is as alone as you can get.

I urge you, however, to include people in all your out-of-town activities during the early days of your grief.

I went off by myself recently to a motel on the edge of Lake Erie. I splashed along the edge of the water, and my room had a Jacuzzi. I'd never been in a motel room with a Jacuzzi before, but I discovered that being alone in a motel room is as alone as you can get. Being alone in a Jacuzzi isn't much fun either.

So don't go on your first vacation by yourself unless it's on a tour where you're automatically a part of a group, or to a conference where people, some of whom are also by themselves, have interests similar to yours. And even then, don't go too soon.

"Hi, I'm Meg Woodson, and my son, Joey, just died," I said to strangers on elevators when I went alone to such a conference. Strangers, out of town for a good time, don't want to hear it.

I got sick, in an intestinal way.

Afraid I would die of starvation alone in my nameless room in that impersonal motel, once a day I called room service, and once a day room service wheeled in a table covered with a white cloth bearing a silver ice bucket on top of which lay—a banana.

Bananas will help what ails me, I thought. I was wrong.

My bill mounted. Snow closed the airport. "Your room is booked. You must vacate," said the manager.

Traveling can create over-the-edge stress for grievers alone and far from home. As soon as I was on my way home to my own bed, however, sickness ceased.

You have awesome survival skills.

So be cautious, but know that grievers have awesome survival skills.

The Toughest Days of Grief

You can use a vacation to strengthen bonds with supportive family and friends; to discover that you can function on your own; to know some measure of happiness without your *love*; to remove yourself from the grind of your grief, from your own deadening; to let nature act as aid and antidote to your sorrow; and, if you desire, to hear your Messiah.

Take a holiday.

You can bear the pain of your special days if you feel pleasure alongside the pain.

Plan Ahead:

As vacation time draws near, gather a few people together in a circle in the woods and ask them to share sad-happy memories of your *love*.

Make a scrapbook of mementos of get-away times you and your *love* had together: theater ticket stub, resort postcard, restaurant napkin, map, autumn leaf, shoelace from child's tennis shoe.

Decorate your breakfast table with a single flower on the day of the week you and your *love* spent special time together.

Take up scuba diving or roller-blading.*

Go out in your backyard at 2 a.m. and whisper the secrets of your grieving heart to God.*

---

* Indicates suggestions appropriate for those bereaved by divorce as well as death.

CHAPTER 3

Sad Days

There is a sense that everything should be fixed
and everything can be fixed. My view is more
that there is pain that has to be lived through.

Dr. Milton Viederman

Like a fingerprint, each person's journey with
grief will vary somewhat. But the general reality
is this: One cannot go around, under or over
grief. One must go through grief by leaning into
the pain to work it out.... Grief work is in
essence a thorough and on-going review process. It takes a long time. It is never fully or
finally accomplished.

Dr. Terry O'Brien

Your birthday . . . your wedding anniversary . . . your graduation day . . . your *love's* death day . . . Labor Day. . . .

Oh, so many special days. Your heart sinks. Lesser holidays. Days that mark the milestones in your life. Days
that commemorate your loss. How will you cope?

Well, let's take the feelings that make these days hard to cope with one feeling at a time, and let's begin with sadness. Some of your special days warrant chapters of their own in this book, and some do not, but sadness—and loneliness and anger and guilt—engulfs you on all your special days.

Name your saddest days. Hold your sadness gently in your hands.

My birthday and wedding anniversary both fall in May. And Memorial Day.

Cars pack the driveways on our street on Memorial Day, and cookout sounds and smells drift out of backyards. The sounds and smells of families come together.

Friends and far-off family include us in their celebrations of Thanksgiving and Christmas, but Memorial Day is like birthdays and anniversaries, a lesser holiday on which others don't know how empty-hearted our empty drive leaves us.

I hate the *merry* month of May.

Birthdays and anniversaries are particularly sad for me because *I* miss *my* children most on the days that mark the milestones of *my* life.

No one is interested in my being a year older the way my children were interested. I don't have the same history of birthdays with anyone else.

Even as a child, my birthday was uniquely my day. Only the birthday girl blew out the candles. Then my children came along, and their birthdays took precedence over mine. Then my children grew up enough to realize that Mama had birthdays, too, and in their artless way they wrapped my birthdays in their love. Those *were* the days.

Our church put on a twenty-fifth wedding anniversary party for Joe and me, but what stands out for me is Peg coming home from college for the event . . . her furtive searching through our albums for a wedding picture to display. She was *ours*. She shared in *our* anniversary as no one else could.

And then last May I received my master's degree in counseling. "I'm only attending graduation because of my children," I heard a fellow graduate say. "I think it's important for them to see what their mother has done."

I withdrew from graduation. I withdrew from the joy-become-sorrow of all my special days.

Joe's birthday comes in May, too. And Mother's Day.

I hate the dreary, dreary, dreary, dreary, dreary, dreary month of May.

The days when you feel most sad may not be the same as mine. Name *your* saddest days. Write them down. Hold your sadness gently in your hands.

Maybe you have no one left who knows when it's your birthday. How forgotten do you feel on the day no one remembers?

Perhaps you numb yourself when your grief-going gets rough. If you don't let yourself feel sad, you won't be sad—you think. I still think that way at times, and it's true that on occasion we grievers need to tone down our feelings lest they gush out of us with such force we spin in out-of-control circles.

Denial has its place. Grief has a life of its own.

But the month of May is not a merry month for me because I stifle that life routinely, because I am tear*y* instead of tear*ful* habitually. I let a few tears slide down my cheeks, but I stifle my sobs. Yet my grief for my children—your grief for your *love*—is so foundational that only floods of tears dislodge it. Only hurricane-sobs wash it away.

If you keep your grief inside you, you keep it inside you. If you let your grief out, you let it out and away. The best thing you can do to get through your saddest days is to feel your sadness.

Oh, you say, but being consumed with my pain is selfish.

Oh, you say, but being consumed with my pain is selfish. If I think of others, I won't be preoccupied with myself.

Oh? Tell yourself that when you have a toothache. If there's decay in your tooth, the only way to get rid of the pain so you can think of anything but the pain is to drill in and get the rotten stuff out.

Oh, you say, but my daughter, my wife, my mother is with God. If I truly loved her, I'd be happy for her instead of sad for me. How can I weep at her grave when that's only her body in the ground?

Oh? Your mother's hand on your shoulder did not en-rich you? Your wife's body in your arms did not exalt you? Her body meant everything to you, the life went out of it, and, presto, it meant nothing to you?

Don't tell me those are only Peggie's and Joey's bodies in the ground. Those bodies came out of my body. Those bodies resembled my body.

Of course I'm happy that my children are with God, but by virtue of that fact, they are not with me.

When Christ came upon a funeral procession for a young man—an only son whose mother was a widow—did He say, "Keep a stiff upper lip, Mother"? Or did He have *compassion* on her, *feel her passion with her*, and give her son back to her?

And when He stood by His friend Lazarus's grave, did Christ smile and say, "Lazarus is better off"? Or did He groan in His spirit, *belch*—according to the original language—as a horse belches from the depths of its in-nards? Not a nice image, the sound and the smell of a horse belching? Well, death is not nice, my fellow-griever, and our sweet-smelling funeral composure is not an ap-propriate response.

I reject churches that rob human beings of human feel-ings. Sorrow is not sin. I condemn homes where parents model stoicism instead of sentiment, where little children are soothed too soon when they cry, where older children are ridiculed or smacked when they cry, until they cannot cry when they try.

Lean into your sadness, my sad, sad fellow-griever.

Oh, you say, but I feel worse after I cry. Stuffed up. Wrung out.

Oh, you say, but my family, my children, worry about me when I cry. I don't want to upset them more than they're already upset. They get angry when I cry.

"What's the hardest part of the divorce for you?" a friend asked Jan's ten-year-old daughter, Carrie.

"Watchin' Mama cry."

"Because you think she'll never stop?"

"No, it's just hard to watch. I know she'll stop because she cried like that when my baby brother died, too, and she stopped then."

"I can't protect Carrie from pain," says Jan, "but already in her young life I've modeled her means of survival."

Oh, you say, but it's so long since my *love* died. I should be over it.

But are you over it? It takes forever to get over the loss of a love.

"The thing that's helped me most since Suzette died," says Sue, "is knowing that I don't have to get over it. I may grow accustomed to missing her, but I will always miss her.

"Carlotta, Suzette's best friend, is four now, but still afraid of *boo-boos*, terrified by the sight of blood, but this is what she said to me: 'I'd give anything to get Suzette back from heaven. I'd even scrape my knees to get her back.

"Suzette died a year ago. A year is a long time when you're four.

The Toughest Days of Grief

"I don't care how long it's been. I'd *scrape my knees* to get Suzette back, too, and it feels good to admit that."

"How do you respond," I asked Gracie, "when someone says you should be over Al's death?"

"Nastily. 'God forbid anything should happen to your husband,' I tell them, 'but if it does, let's see how quick you get over it.'"

Go easy on yourself. You've a well inside you filled to the brim with your grief, and every time you cry, really cry, you empty the well out. But the well fills again, and you must repeat and repeat the emptying-out process.

The level of sorrow in your *well* lessens as time passes, but it never runs dry, and there are always birthdays and anniversaries, those most-sorrowful days when the well fills to its brim as at the beginning. And the main thing you can do to get yourself through these special occasions is to: weep, sob, lament at the top of your lungs—lift up your head and howl.

Oh, you say, but I always feel worse after I cry. Stuffed up. Wrung out.

Well, you may feel worse at first, but then you will feel better. Catharsis is the best feeling in the world.

Nothing compares to being raised from the half-dead into a springtime of redbud and dogwood.

If you don't experience catharsis, two things will happen.

One, you will get sick, over and over. God made tear ducts so you could find physical and emotional relief from the tension of pent-up emotions. When you do not use your God-given release system, all the other systems of your body go out of kilter, and the first system to go is your immune system.

And, two, you will get depressed. Depression is not sadness, though you may be sad and depressed at the same time. Depression is a sense of hopelessness and helplessness that pervades your life.

Of course, you'll get sick and depressed from crying all the time as well as none of the time. Then, too, some depression is a natural part of grief: your sense, for example, that there's no point in looking for someone new to love because everyone you love will die. Your preoccupation with death will lessen as your grief lessens.

What happens when you get depressed from unwept-out grief, however, is that when you depress one emotion, you depress all emotions with it. As a result, you go about in an on-going, half-dead emotional state. Nothing gives you pleasure.

I know about depression from personal experience because I could not cry after Joey died. I could not sleep. I was tired all the time—and down. How I regret that I stayed shut down for the rest of Peggie's life.

"Kids are always asking me why I'm so chipper," she said to me once, "and, ya know, I think the reason is that I'm in rebellion against the way you are, Mother.

"If you're a kid, Mother, and you're in a house, and something's wrong in the house, whose fault are you gonna think it is? How do you think it makes me feel that you're always tired because of me?"

Four years after Joey died, my accumulation of depressed feelings took over, and I spent the better part of a year in bed, in the dark, covered with sweat at any exertion. Peg was away at college, and I was glad she was out of it, though sorry for what I put Joe through.

I cry now even when I don't want to, but I wouldn't go back to the way I was for anything—because now *I feel alive.*

I lived with low-grade depression before Joey died. Probably I would have lived that way until I died, but the depression that resulted from the deaths of my children compounded my chronic depression until I *had* to feel my feelings—or feel no feelings.

Nothing compares to being raised from the half-dead into a springtime of redbud and dogwood. I would not have chosen that my children die for the good that has come to me, but they did die, and I have been resurrected.

Nothing is wrong with you if you can't cry; you've just been programmed not to.

Some people grieve spontaneously. Watch a Middle Eastern man shake his fist in the air as his fallen son is carried home. Listen to the keening of an Oriental woman as she throws herself on her husband's wasted body. Even in this country some people give way to unrestrained sorrow.

"I'm a real emotional person," says Gracie. "Give me a dog story and I cry. I have a friend whose husband is in a nursing home with Alzheimer's. I cry over the phone with her at ten-thirty at night if something's buggin' me, and she cries with me, too. I know who I can cry with and who I can't."

Nothing is wrong with you if you can't cry; you've just been programmed not to. Reprogramming yourself may take time, but you can do it. Crying is as natural as breathing.

Are you like Gracie, or do you have to make grief happen on deeper and deeper levels? If you do, here are some suggestions that may help. Pick one or two that are right for you.

Just think, one person's undivided, caring, professional attention one hour a week.

See a therapist.

A good therapist will support you as you express your feelings in a way people in your everyday world—whose world your grief is turning upside down—cannot. Just think, a therapist offers you one person's undivided, caring, professional attention one hour a week.

"What happens to your body when you visit Peggie's grave?" my therapist asked. "Well, what would happen to your body if you let anything happen to it? Would your knees wobble? Your stomach heave?" A good therapist knows what questions to ask to call forth your feelings.

"Verbal people use words to avoid feelings, Meg. Talking about feelings is different than feeling feelings." A good therapist pinpoints your defenses and guides you past them.

"What happened to you when you cried as a child, Meg?" A good therapist helps you work through past experience with feelings.

"Yes, Meg, I know you're afraid that if you start crying, you won't stop. But you will. I promise."

Dr. Alan D. Wolfelt, Director of the Center for Loss and Life Transition in Fort Collins, Colorado, tells of a client who sits at her kitchen table every day at 5:00 P.M. and waits for her deceased husband to walk through the garage door.

Friends say, "Keep busy doing something else at the time Larry came home." . . . "Get a job." . . . "Move to Florida."

"I tell her to listen for her husband's car," says Dr. Wolfelt, "to watch for the door to open. She'll cry every day when her husband doesn't walk through the garage door, and in time she'll *know* that he will not walk back to her through any door and she'll *reconcile* herself *to* her loss." Dr. Wolfelt never says *recover from*.

"I tell another widow to sit in her husband's closet and smell his suits," he says.

Most people *say* you need to cry but are uncomfortable when you do. They admire how you're doing only when your eyes are dry. A good therapist will use all your senses to help you *smell* and *taste* and *touch* your grief.

At the time I saw my therapist, I wasn't able to cry in front of him, but when I left his office, I cried like the third little piggie, wee-wee-wee, all the way home.

I am still uplifted by the recognition I saw in every face.

Join a group.

"I know intellectually now what my feelings are about my parents' abuse of me as a child," Ted said after we'd worked together for several weeks, "but I can't feel my feelings. How do I get them from my head to my heart?"

"Join a group."

And after twelve sessions of group, "I've cried more for my lost childhood in the past twelve weeks," Ted said, "than in the rest of my twenty-four years."

In a group, you listen to others talk about their pain, your throat tightens, and before you know it, you're choking out your own.

Once when I fell apart in a group and embarrassment overwhelmed me, the leader said, "Look into the face of each person here." It was the last thing I wanted to do, but I made my swollen eyes connect with every pair of eyes in the circle. I am still uplifted when I think about the *recognition* I saw in every face.

Oh, but I'm a private person, you say. I couldn't handle a group situation, especially now.

Well, I'm introverted, too. I see my quietness as a strength, my love of solitude an asset as a writer—but a liability as a griever.

Grief work is agonizing work; you need all the cheering squads you can get. One of the good things that can come from the extremity of your grief is an exploration of your shadow, extroverted side.

Here, look at these pictures of Tracy and me on Fourth of Julys past.

Reminisce with a friend.

The important thing is that you talk to someone. Talking to yourself as a griever helps. But say the words to someone other, and they take on new reality.

Ask clearly for what you need. "If you want to help me get through Valentine's Day, let me tell you what I miss about Tim on Valentine's Day."

"Let me reminisce. Here, look at these pictures of Tracy and me on Fourth of Julys past."

Don't, of course, talk about your loss with every person you meet. People will stop asking you to parties. A good cry can ward off the blues, but so can a belly laugh.

Sense what different friends are able to give you, and ask clearly for what you need from each. You *may* get it.

Locate the muscles where your grief is bunched up and get them unbunched.

See a physical therapist.

If you store up your feelings in your spirit, you store them up in your body as well. Locate the muscles where your grief is *bunched up* and get them *unbunched*. When these muscles become fluid, your feelings will more readily pour out.

I stored my feelings up in my shoulder muscles. "I work on the Cleveland Browns," my physical therapist told me. "Their muscles are the only muscles I've worked on that are harder than yours." Each time I left her office I gulped for air from a deeper place than I'd breathed from before, and cried from a deeper place than I'd cried from before.

After I'd been seeing my physical therapist for several weeks, a friend looked on my nicely sloping shoulders and said, "My goodness, Meg, you have a neck."

Many people survive their losses without professional help of any kind. I was strong on therapy because I wanted not just to reconcile myself to my losses but to use them to grow to wholeness.

We find what solace we can—most likely in the habit of our choice.

Quit your habit.

Another thing you can do to release your emotions, with or without professional help, is to control your addictions, no matter what form they take. Drinking or gambling compulsively or even talking nonstop—most people in our society have at least one addiction.

Addictions numb feelings. Numbing feelings is what addictions do, and when we think we cannot bear our feelings, we find what solace we can—anywhere—most likely in the habit of our choice.

"I started smoking when my father died," says John. "I was sixteen. By the time my mother died last year, I'd been smoking two packs of cigarettes a day for twenty-six years. I felt better when I lit up, but before long I felt more depressed than ever.

"I kept yelling, 'I'm an orphan. I'm a forty-eight-year-old orphan,' but I didn't shed a tear."

This year John joined a structured stop-smoking program—grievers need structure. And as he stopped smoking, to his amazement, his tears for both parents rolled.

Yes, yes, you say, I'll quit my habit when the worst of my grief is over.

No, no, the time is now.

You invite books to talk to you when you want their company, and shut their covers when you don't.

Read a book.
Books make good company when you're grieving. You invite books to talk to you when you want their company; you *shut their covers* when you don't.

Books that explain the nature of grief reassure you. Ah, you sigh, my curious, copious, headache-producing, put-me-to-bed tears are normal. I can let them fall.

Books that tell of other people's triumph over grief inspire you. Ah, you sigh, one day I will inspire others. And the hope that one day you will not hurt as you hurt now supports your tears for how you hurt now.

Think of a novel that makes you cry every time you read it. *Old Yeller?* Read it again. You'll begin by crying for a boy and his dog, but not for long.

Or if reading requires too much concentration, watch a movie that makes you cry every time you see it. Watch *A Night to Remember* on video in your home and cry as conspicuously as you want.

You may find poetry with its imagery and intensity of feeling helpful. A favorite poem to read on my saddest days is Matthew Arnold's "Dover Beach":

> *The sea is calm tonight,*
> *The tide is full, the moon lies fair*
> *Upon the straits. . . .*
> *Listen! You hear the grating roar*
> *Of pebbles which the waves draw back, and fling,*
> *At their return, up the high strand.*
> *Begin, and cease, and then again begin,*
> *With tremulous cadence slow, and bring*
> *The eternal note of sadness in.*

There goes my reason for living. There goes the one I adore.

Listen to music.

You may find poetry put to music even more moving. I once asked a hymn writer to write a hymn people could be sad with.

"You mean a hymn that starts out sad and ends up happy?"

"No, I mean a hymn that starts out sad and ends up sad, that lets me be with God in my sadness."

"Oh," he said, "you mean a hymn that starts out sad and ends up happy?"

Some people are so eager to praise God for His mercies that their tenor notes drown out our bass miseries.

"Al and I went to every Roger Whitaker concert that came to town," says Gracie. "After Al died I made a tape of the songs we liked best. I feel nostalgic-sad when I listen to it. Engelbert Humperdinck helps, too. *There goes my reason for living. There goes my everything.* I turn the music up really loud and get really emotional inside. This is the way *I* feel."

What music gets you emotional? "Sleepin' Single in a Double Bed"? Brahms' "German Requiem"?

Write a tribute to your love in longhand and tie it together with yarn.

Give creative expression to your grief.

Any form of self-expression expresses the grief that is so much a part of yourself.

I suggested to Ted that he keep a sad/angry journal to express his feelings toward his abusive parents. He came in the next week with twenty-two reasons he was sad/angry at mother, fourteen reasons he was sad/angry at father, and ten reasons he was sad/angry at father and mother together.

He went through his lists with such an eruption of emotion, it frightened even me. Yet it cleansed him. Would his feelings have been that specific or real had he not first put them down in black and white?

Write about the outward mechanics of your *love's* dying and about your inner *workings* as you watched the outward mechanics. Most people don't want you to respeak such details, but you can rewrite and rewrite them.

Write a tribute to your *love* in longhand, tie it together with yarn, and distribute it to family and friends. Write a one-page memorial, maybe a sonnet, and send it out with your Christmas letter.

Distill the essence of your *love* in one sentence and put it in cross-stitch.

Dance your feelings. Paint your feelings. Build a memorial to your *love* in wood.

Express—expel—your feelings.

I feel so much better, now I can cry, and now that I can cry, I feel so much better.

Take an antidepressant.

Jim, our seventy-year-old widower, came to see me three years after his wife's death. He had not cried when she died, nor since, though he had tried, and though his whole life had centered on his Ora. He was so depressed he could not take out the trash or wash his hair.

I recommended antidepressant medication, but Jim said, "I should be able to get on top of this myself. I pray for God's help. I don't want to be dependent on drugs. My nose will get red if I cry."

He couldn't buy a loaf of bread, but he wouldn't cry because *his nose would get red?*

After six weeks on drug therapy, Jim said, "I feel so much better, now I can cry, and now that I can cry, I feel so much better."

Don't rule out any healing option. Let the special sadness of your special days push you into action.

Welcome grief whenever it knocks on the door of your heart as indispensable—a friend.

"It's not the holidays, the expected days, that do me in," says Jan. "It's the *Tuesdays* when I'm congratulating myself on how far I've come, and then I check the single box on some form and it's all back."

You, too, may find that your saddest days are not always special-occasion days. It may be the day the doctor says your gall bladder has to come out. Being alone in a hospital room is right up there with being alone in a motel room. Or the day you get a promotion at work and there's no one you *belong to* to go home to and tell.

Grief is not the enemy. Whenever it knocks on the door of your heart, welcome grief as indispensable—a friend.

"I hate to go in Joey's room," Peg, a young fourteen, said after his death. "I mean, every time I go in Joey's room, it's like he ought to be in there. Ya know, with him wearin' his glasses over the sides of his ears instead of over the tops, workin' on one of his three-thousand-piece puzzles.

"I mean, every time I go in Joey's room, I cry. But then when I come out, I feel better."

"I remember a Tuesday morning," says Jan, "maybe six months after Craig left, when every person who came into my office talked about someone who was having a baby, or about schedule conflicts with mates, or about birthday celebrations.

"On the stroke of noon, I bolted out to my car and began screaming. I couldn't believe the sound was coming from me. I got home, into the hallway, fell on my knees exhausted and sobbed.

"Craig was seeing *her* long before I knew it. Even my memories were gone. So much work to survive when I didn't want to survive without *him*.

"Until checking all the *single boxes* of your life becomes routine, each unexpected reminder of your married life leaves you rejected again, divorced again."

"Would you have reached the ease of sorrow you know now, Jan, if you hadn't first felt such depths of sorrow?"

"Just feeling my sorrow wouldn't have done it, but nothing else would have done it without feeling my sorrow."

You'll begin to reconcile yourself to your loss, my fellow-griever, not when a month or six months or a year has passed, but when you begin to feel your sadness around your loss.

Cry, baby. Cry.

You can bear the pain of your special days if you feel pleasure alongside the pain.

You can bear the pain of your special days if you feel the pain.

Plan Ahead:

Make an appointment to talk with your *love's* doctor or nurse on the first anniversary of *his* death.

Imagine your *love* sitting across from you in an empty chair and say "thank you" for ways *she* was there for you on birthdays past.

Set a place for your *love* on your Memorial Day picnic table. Place a lighted candle on the plate and ask guests to observe a moment of silence.

Create one hour without pain for yourself on your *love's* death day or on the day your divorce became final.*

Sit quietly in a comfortable chair. Imagine the door to the room opening and yourself as a child coming in. The child looks wounded. Reach out your arms to *your wounded child* and ask why he is hurting. Hold him and encourage him to cry.*

---

* Indicates suggestions appropriate for those bereaved by divorce as well as death.

CHAPTER 4

Lonely Days

The human spirit seems inherently allergic to isolation. It cannot abide a sense of being permanently alone or stranded in all the vastness of the universe or lost in the midst of the complexities of personal experience.

Howard Thurman

"Anything you do deeply is very lonely. . . ."
"Are you lonely?" I asked him.
"Of course," he answered. "But I do not let it toss me away. It is just loneliness."

Natalie Goldberg, *Wild Mind*

*H*aving finished the last chapter, you may ask, "That's it? Cry?"

Well, crying your feelings out is the most practical advice I can give you for your saddest or your loneliest days.

Even the word *lonely* has a lonely sound. A forlorn feeling. Tears drip from the word.

Maybe you were lonely all your life until Cathy or Carl came along. What is it like to come to the end of the end of your loneliness?

You have a lot to cry about.

Yet if crying is the only advice I give you for your loneliest days, it's disastrous advice.

You can bear the pain of your special days if you feel pleasure alongside the pain.

You can bear the pain of your special days if you feel the pain.

And—

You can bear the pain of your special days if you feel the pain with people.

It feels good to know you can bear your pain. It feels good to bear it.

With people. Hear me, my lonely, grieving friend—*with people.*

Yes, you may want to spend some of your special days alone, parts of them alone, but these days cast a harsh spotlight on your loneliness. Why hibernate through them? Why create unnecessary loneliness for yourself on your necessarily lonely days?

I validate your feelings of double desertion—by one person in death and by other people in life.

Jennie, a young client whose fiancée broke their engagement, says, "I can't think about anything but Jeremy, can't talk about anything but Jeremy . . . but . . . I just heard that . . . Jeremy's seeing someone else.

"My best friend says, 'Oh, stop feeling sorry for yourself. I have a friend who'd be perfect for you. Get on with your life.'

"But I don't want anyone but Jeremy, and I keep having mood swings, and sometimes I'm so tired I can't get out of bed, and sometimes I feel like I can't breathe. Am I going crazy?"

"Is any day special to your relationship with Jeremy coming up?"

"Well, maybe Friday. Friday would have been my *weddin' day*."

Poor Jennie, for not having her feelings validated.

Poor me, when a casual friend changes direction when she sees me coming down the supermarket aisle. She doesn't know what to say to me, but, still, poor me.

Poor you, when good friends avoid you at parties. They don't want to think about their own mortality, but, still, poor you, standing in a corner staring into your Taster's Choice.

Sometimes even family members are so afraid they'll say or do the wrong thing, they don't say or do anything.

I validate your feelings of double desertion—by one person in death and by other people in life. We grievers are not responsible for all our loneliness.

Every time one of us makes the tiniest splash, the other one goes under.

"We're like two drowning people," Joe said in the early days of our grief for Joey, "each treading water for all we're worth to keep our noses above the surface, and every time one of us makes a tiny splash, the other one goes under."

We want too much. No one can replace our loved one. No one can become our lost one. We demand comfort of each other but are unable even to comfort ourselves.

We're lost. And undone. And we *splash* automatically; we grab and clutch and kick everyone close enough to us to splash, especially on our loneliest *would have been our weddin' days*.

It's the stuff of which further loss is made: the divorce of surviving parents, the estrangement of divorced parent from child, the fights between surviving brothers and sisters.

We grievers are responsible for some of our loneliness.

So . . . how do we splash, and what can we do to keep our splashing to a minimum?

Why can't my husband grieve the right way—my way?

"You'd feel better if you'd get out and visit the congregation with me," Joe said after Peggie's death.

"No, Joe, I'd feel better if you'd go out to dinner with me, just the two of us together."

Joe, the extrovert, replenishes his emotional batteries by being with people, the more people the better, however casual the contact. I, the introvert, replenish my emotional batteries in solitude or in intimate one-on-one contacts. Being with lots of people drains me.

Every time Joe said, "If you'd just visit the congregation with me," I wanted to yell, "Is that how little you know me? How can you insist that I do something that exhausts me, as exhausted as I am already?"

Compassionate Friends is a support group for parents who have lost children. "It's lonely going to Compassionate Friends alone," Joe said.

I tried going with him, but while Joe exulted in the healing that resulted from listening to bereaved parents share their stories, I, who tend to take other people's pain on as my own, ended up in bed after each meeting.

"I need to talk about Tommy," a mother laments, "but Big Tom won't talk. He won't even listen. He's built a wall around himself I can't get through."

"I know people grieve differently," she says, but the resentment sounding through her words sends another message: Why can't my husband grieve the right way—my way?

Well, people *are* different. Women tend to cry in the car when they're grieving; men tend to scream. Women long for sexual tenderness, for emotional oneness; men tend to become either impotent or sexually aggressive.

We are all so different in so many ways, demanding that others grieve the way we grieve is one of the ways we splash.

It's hard, I know. You want to be glued to the person you have left in every thought and action, but I urge you, hang in there with your *Big Tom*. Self-esteem plummets with the loss of love; neither of you can handle much criticism right now. Think about ways you are there for each other.

Your needs are enormous. Look to a variety of people to get them met. Look to yourself.

My car stalled on a bridge today, Meg, and I had this incredible urge to leap off.

"I wanted to leap off the top of Perry's Monument," Joe told me, aghast, a few weeks after Peggie died. "I'd just paid my money to go up, but I got out of there fast."

And a couple weeks after that, "My car stalled on a bridge today, Meg, and I had this incredible urge to leap off."

"What was that about, Joe?"

"Just a way to get away from the pain, Meg, that's all, just a way to get away from the pain."

"One day I'm on top of the world, and the next day I'm so low I can't get out of bed," wails poor Jennie.

"Well, your despair is so deep, Jennie, the only way you can get on top of it is to rise to unnatural heights. Then, since you can't maintain heights that high, you fall to even lower depths. No, you don't have bipolar depression, though temporarily your symptoms are similar."

Unfortunately, the behavior that makes us grievers crazy makes the people around us crazy, too. It dampens their desire to be around us a whole lot. My fear that Joe had cast himself off some parapet every time he was late coming home from work did not enhance my relationship with Joe.

Our crazy-making behavior is a second way we splash.

So explain to those around you that your irritability or lethargy or aches and pains are normal in the abnormal circumstances of your loss and grief, that you won't go on in your confused or fearful state permanently. The people with whom you live and work need all the reassurance they can get.

And so do you. Grief itself feels a lot like fear.

But, then, do what you can do to control your out-of-controlness.

Look at a sun-red sky. Meditate. Listen to Mendelssohn. Go bowling. See an old movie with an old friend. Do whatever you used to like to do.

Get yourself back. What do you believe in? What are you good at? You've lost your *love*; don't lose yourself, too.

When I want to achieve internal balance, I balance my checkbook: a brief, precise, manageable task with a beginning and an end, that gives me a sense of accomplishment, that brings order to the chaos of my checkbook and my inner life.

Of course, balancing your checkbook may be the last thing you should do to center yourself! Determine what connects *you* with *your* core.

All those "don't cares" you exhaled—he inhaled.

Unipolar depression—shutting off feelings—turns on negative feelings in family and friends. People don't take kindly to rejection. No matter what they *know* the cause of your depression is, what they *feel* is your lack of feeling toward them.

Our most pernicious splashing is our most passive splashing; it takes place in numbing waters.

When her sister's long dying from cancer was over, Amanda, a young married woman, converted the den in her home into a second bedroom and closeted herself there every day when she came home from work, echoing her refrains: "I don't care about anything." . . . "I don't care about anybody." . . . "Nobody cares about me."

After six months of shutting herself off this way, Amanda came to see me. "It's Dan, my husband. He's moved in with another woman. Oh, Meg, how could he do this to me?"

Oh, Mandy, how could he not? All those *don't cares* you exhaled—he inhaled.

Remember that grief is feeling your feelings and depression is not feeling your feelings. Move as quickly as you can from depression to the hurricane sobs of the last chapter.

But while you are still *down*, be clear with those around you, verbally and with whatever emotion you can muster, that you are not *down on them*.

"Why didn't Dan come into my room and beg me to come out?"

"Oh, Mandy, you might as well have taped a KEEP OUT sign on your door."

While you may need to spend extra time alone with yourself these days, don't overdo it. Isolation leads to depression and depression to further isolation.

My writing office was in my home before Peggie died, but after she died I rented an office outside my home—a gigantic undertaking at the time—reading the want ads, looking at offices, moving furniture.

I spent three years in my out-of-the-house office writing *Turn It Into Glory,* a book about the last six weeks of Peggie's life. It took every penny I made to pay the rent on my office, so I *had* to get there, *had* to get up in the morning, *had* to comb my hair.

I *had* to get out of the house, and before I got to the corner of my street, I felt my depression lift, even when to that moment I didn't know I was depressed.

Gracie, in her sixties, took a part-time job in telemarketing after Al died. "Talkin' on the phone," says Gracie, "is the only thing I'm good at."

"Don't go to work today," number one son tells her. "You're not feeling up to it today."

"Why should I go to work when I feel up to it?" says Gracie. "I go to work when I don't feel up to it."

I'm weak. I'm weak, self-pity weeps. Fix me. Fix me.

We grievers often use unsportsmanlike tactics to get our needs met, and self-pity is one of the sneakiest—a fourth and favorite way we splash.

Leo Buscaglia says that we recognize the self-pitier by the way he sighs, voice sinking octave by octave, *I'm all alone—again—naturally.*

Self-pity goes on and on and doesn't want to end. *I'm weak, I'm weak*, self-pity weeps, *fix me, fix me.*

Pathologically caring people join in pity parties, but they produce anger in healthy people. "If you loved me, I wouldn't have to ask for your help," the self-pitier whines, and therein lies his defeat, because love cannot be forced.

I recognize myself here, particularly after Joey died. "If you were plain sad, Mother, that would be one thing," a teenage Peggie yelled, "but long-suffering is a lot worse."

Pitying yourself is tricky because it feels somewhat like being loved, but within yourself you know which you are being.

If you settle for being pitiful, it's because you don't believe you're lovable.

So . . . are you lovable?

Say *yes.*

Nor certitude, nor peace, nor help for pain.

A fifth way we grievers splash is by exaggerating the loneliness we feel without our *love* into a cosmic loneliness.

"My family can be so *un*helpful when I'm sick," Gracie cries, shut in with the flu. "Number two son says, 'You've come a long way since Pop died,' but he doesn't know what it's like when I'm alone in bed at night and my head and chest hurt so bad, I grab a pillow and cuddle it.

"Al would know how I feel, I think. And then I go all the way back and want my mother to put her arms around me."

"Is this how you feel, Gracie?" I ask, and read her the second verse of Matthew Arnold's "Dover Beach":

> The Sea of Faith
> Was once, too, at the full, and round earth's shore
> Lay like the folds of a bright girdle furl'd.
> But now I only hear
> Its melancholy, long, withdrawing roar . . .
>   for the world, which seems
> To lie before us like a land of dreams,
> So various, so beautiful, so new,
> Hath really neither joy, nor love, nor light,
> Nor certitude, nor peace, nor help for pain;
> And we are here as on a darkling plain. . . .

When you're grieving, anything that can be construed as a rejection elevates your sense of abandonment by your lost *love* to a sense of abandonment by all your *loves*. Store this fact away in a corner of your mind, and when *the big loneliness* descends, bring the fact out and ask it to penetrate your darkness.

Or you may have to wait out the darkness—your PMS, your spouse's anger, a friend's busy spell, Labor Day, Halloween, a friend's wedding, your flu-fever—knowing on some level of consciousness that when the heat in your body breaks, so will the heat that brands your soul ALL ALONE.

Mandy comes to see me week after week now wailing, "I'M ALL ALONE," her voice hollow with woe.

"But you talk about being close to your niece, Mandy. And what about the people in your Alanon program?"

"I live alone," wails Mandy.

"Well, that's what you should say then. That's hard, but *I live alone* is different from *I'M ALL ALONE*."

"If Dan would come back," wails Mandy, "I wouldn't be ALL ALONE."

"I understand that that is the way you feel, Mandy. It's awful, isn't it?"

When you're grieving and you don't think well of yourself to begin with, it's easy to make that leap from *I no longer have my husband* to *I no longer have anyone* to *I'm not the kind of person anyone will ever want to have*.

So . . . what does your loneliness say about you? What does your loneliness not say?

Anyone who attacked my base could take a hike.

A word of caution. No, you don't want to cause people to back away from you, but there may be a person or two from whom you need to back away.

"Before my divorce," says Jan, "I was so accustomed to criticism from everyone in my family, I assumed their criticism was correct. Craig's leaving knocked me so off balance, I thought I'd never have balance again, but my motive was to be okay. I selected relationships that moved me along to okayness. Anyone who attacked my base could take a hike.

"Like Cousin Jane. When I told Cousin Jane that Craig was leaving me for another woman, 'Oh, my,' she said, not missing a beat, 'do you think it's all those meetings you go to?' And, then, 'Oh, well, there's no use crying over spilled milk.'

"We couldn't have a conversation without her lecturing me for my faults or writing off my pain with cliches.

"Shortly after Craig left, my foot went through the floor of my car. Cousin Jane gave me money for another car, but her money did not buy her a license to judge my life.

"I finally told Cousin Jane that just for now I could not connect with someone who constantly compared Craig and me and the woman Craig left me for to my detriment.

"'It's plain to see why Craig left,' said Cousin Jane. 'Well, you'll have to pull yourself up by your own bootstraps.'"

It's hard to break off a relationship that has nurtured you, however dysfunctionally, when you've lost a relationship essential to you. It's also easy to blast to kingdom come everyone who's not the perfect comforter. So act with restraint. But when a relationship feels like an eighteen-wheeler pressing down on your breast bone—act.

May Day! May Day!

Last year I could not face another lonely May, and I confided my need to a friend. My friend sent a card on my birthday, left flowers outside my front door on Mother's Day, invited Joe and me to a cookout on Memorial Day.

A lot of people want to help when you're grieving; they just don't know what you want them to do or when you want them to do it.

But a strange thing happened last May. When I made my need known to one person, an amazing array of people moved in on my special days, as though God had been waiting for me to move before He moved in my behalf.

Early after Peggie's death in times of great despair, *Please, God*, I prayed, *let someone call*. And the phone rang. But later God, like any good father, aided my growth by not doing for me what I could do for myself.

This year I shouted *May Day!* in a different way. I gave parties. Two big ones. Printed invitations. Flowers. An article in the paper.

Okay, several years had passed since Peggie's death, and I gave the parties in April, and they were autograph parties for a new book, but, still, wallflower that I'd always been, I never thought I'd see such a *May*.

What if no one comes? I worried, but I took the risk. I took the initiative. I asked people into my life, and they came in. How good it was.

And then, the morning after the second party—I was so high—the phone rang and a voice in Florida, a stranger's voice, told me my mother had died.

Just like that?

If the death of a child is the most unnatural of deaths, the death of a mother is the most elemental. No one will ever wait for me to call or visit the way my mother waited. No one will sacrifice for me the way my mother sacrificed. No one else has been with me from the beginning. My mother's love was impaired—she was human—but it was a mother's love.

I didn't think I'd forgotten the pain of a new grief, but I had forgotten—the uncivilized pain of a gash slashed top to bottom of my soul.

People who haven't lost a parent think that such loss is natural, inevitable, not to be grieved as other losses. *What do they know?*

Every May as my birthday drew near, my legally blind mother got on her electric scooter and scooted off to the card shop, peering through the cards with her magnifying glass till she found just the right *For My Daughter On Her Birthday* card.

Every year as she grew older and my card came, her once proud penmanship scrawled every-which-way on the envelope, *Save this card* a voice whispered. *Next year no card may come.* . . .

Joe and I celebrated our birthdays and our anniversary this May in a swing at the edge of Lake Erie watching the sun set, but even then we celebrated together. I was not alone.

One thing I learned this year on my special days was that if I cried in front of Joe, or with Joe's arms around me, I felt more cleansed of my grief than if I cried alone.

I had another graduation day this May, my last. It fell on Mother's Day. Now this year not only was I not a mother, I did not have a mother, but I went to graduation. We sang Kermit the Frog's "It's in every one of us to be wise," and the faculty hugged us as they gave us our diplomas, and a fellow-graduate or two asked how I was doing, and it was good.

It felt good—especially this year—to take the initiative not to be alone on my Days in May.

Take heart, my lonely fellow-grievers. Commit yourself to love.

It may be that the pain of having lost someone you loved is so great that you, like Jennie, are saying, "I can't trust *a man* again. I won't risk loving and losing again."

"My birthday is hard without Al," says Gracie, "so this year I had lunch at Denny's. Denny's gives you lunch free on your birthday. Then I went to a car wash where they give you a free exterior car wash on your birthday. I know it doesn't mean much, but they say *Happy Birthday* to you there, too.

"Then I spent the afternoon with my grandson. Marky runs at me yelling, 'I love you, Grandma,' and I just better catch him. I take it for all it's worth every minute I can get it. I know that one day he won't run to me like that, but if I take him now every chance I have, when that time comes, I will have had him."

We grievers risk loss every time we hold out our arms to *catch another*, but the alternative is empty arms.

"When I left Marky," Gracie concluded, "I didn't feel like goin' home alone, so I called the friend I cry with and we went to The Steak House for dinner. They give you a free dinner on your birthday at The Steak House.

"Recently my friend had a stroke. She hardly knows who I am anymore. I cry alone now, for her as well as Al. But I did have her. I'm glad I had her."

Take heart, my lonely fellow-griever. Lean out of your loneliness.

When Peggie died, Joe said, "Okay, Meg, we're what we have left, and one thing we're going to do to enhance our relationship is go away together once a month overnight."

"We can't afford to do that, Joe."

"We can't afford not to do that, Meg."

We found an inn, the Inn at Honey Run, and we have gone away overnight almost every month since Peggie's death. We walk for miles along country roads. We sit on a hill and watch sheep graze.

Once a month we leave our over-stimulating, workaholic, relationship-deadening lives and cleave only to each other.

I thought recently that I might have to have a mastectomy. Panic-stricken, I asked, "Will you be there at the moment they wheel me down to surgery, Joe? Will you be there at the moment they bring me back?"

"I'll be there."

"If I die, will you be there at the moment of my death?" Talk about melodrama—and in the middle of the night.

"I'll be there, Meg."

I tell you, at times of deepest grief, the strife within each of us was so harsh, the strife between us was so harsh, we could have separated—and where would I be now without Joe's *I'll be there?*

Think may times, my fellow-griever, before you inflict permanent damage on a cherished relationship in a period of frenzied grief.

Relationships that were in trouble before your loss will be in greater trouble after your loss. You may not want to preserve them, but if you do, you'll have to work at changing them. You've lost the love of the one who is gone; don't, by default, lose the love of those you have left.

Take heart, my lonely fellow-griever. Lean into relationships.

Commit yourself to love.

Plan Ahead:

Take money left in your *love's* wallet and eat out on your wedding anniversary with a friend—compliments of *him*.

Hold a baby on Mother's Day.

Put a candle in a window and light it every night for a week before your *love's* death day. Arrange with a friend or two to do the same.

Volunteer at a hospital or a soup kitchen or a children's home on the day of the week when you feel most alone.*

Sign up for a group activity that requires regular attendance: a softball team, a play-goers' club, a computer class for credit.*

---

* Indicates suggestions appropriate for those bereaved by divorce as well as death.

CHAPTER 5

Angry Days

Only the weak are afraid of emotion, vulnerability, and display of their own humanity.
Taylor Caldwell, *Bright Flows the River*

If you pretend you have no anger and try to bury it, it can bury you. . . . If you let it out in the wrong way, it can ruin your marriage, alienate your children, or get you fired. . . . If you somehow turn it around on yourself, it can tear your self-image apart.
Neil Clark Warren

When Al died," cries Gracie, "a part of me died. I feel so empty. I miss him. I miss him."

Yes, sorrow and loneliness are an integral part of grief for everyone—and so is anger.

Oh, you say, but no one was to blame for my *love's* death. How can I be angry when there's no one to be angry at?

Easily.

Joey and I walked down the street one summer day, hands clasped, arms swinging high between us, and the next day he lay still and white in a hospital bed groaning with every breath. "I don't suppose—you could—put me out of my misery—could you—Mama?"

He asked that, my innocent son.

We never walked down a summer road again.

I came home from the hospital without him—forevermore without him—assumed a boxer's stance, punched the air, my anger only intensified because there was no one to punch.

Angry at injustice. Angry at their physical pain. Angry at our emotional pain.

"I still feel overwhelming rage for the way Mark died," says Maryanne, whose son died of muscular dystrophy. "I'm an adult child of an alcoholic. I like to be in control, but Mark's death was so awful. Senseless. And all I could do was watch."

Yes, we grievers are angry people. Angry at injustice. Angry at their physical pain. Angry at our emotional pain. Angry at death's unlimited power over us all.

"You know how depressed I've been the past few days?" I asked Joe early this morning.

"Well, I'm not depressed anymore, and you know why? Because I'm angry. I'm angry at Sally for turning her back to me in church and asking the person next to me out for coffee. And I'm angry at Dr. Moore for giving me a robe that wouldn't go all the way around ... move over, will you, Joe? You always hog more than your share of the bed.

"And you know who else I'm angry at? I'm angry at my mother for not calling me before she died. They found her body in the chair beside her phone. She called the doctor, but did she call Emily or me? No. How dare she die without saying good-bye?

"But you know what I'm most angry about? I'm angry *that* she died. Oh, Joe, she was ... my mother. She should not have ... left me."

Illogical? Yes. But no bundle of feelings as big and mixed up as grief is logical.

We grievers are the angriest people in the world.

He didn't act like a man; he acted like a jerk.

We're angry at people who weren't there for us in the way we wanted them to be when our *love* died. One man I know of is angry seventeen years later because the nurse who stood beside him when his wife died didn't touch him.

We're angry at people who weren't there for us in any way when our *love* died. A minister, in a longstanding support group with Joe, didn't come to the hospital during the six weeks it took Peg to die. "If I had just been on the east side," he said later, "I would have stopped by."

What? The east side is twenty-five minutes away.

We're angry at people who bear responsibility for our *love's* death.

Al and Gracie sold their house shortly before Al died. The basement hadn't leaked for the twenty-five years they lived there, but it leaked for the new owners almost at once. The new owners brought legal action against Al— knowing of his tentative hold on life. Day after day they harassed him, till Al's doctor volunteered to testify that they contributed to Al's death.

We're angry at people who weren't good comforters after our *love's* death.

"Brian, my husband, didn't hug me at Mark's funeral," says Maryanne, "but he hugged everybody else like it was party time. He didn't act like a man; he acted like a jerk. *Oh, boy, oh, boy, more pretty women to hug.*

"I got less caring from him than you'd expect from a neighbor, but I got anger from him, as though he were saying, *I put you in charge. You let this happen.*

"He cussed Mark out at home. He rarely visited him in the hospital, but six weeks after Mark died, he became *the wounded father.*

"Even Amy, my best friend for twenty years, wanted me *over it* right away. 'You're not doing well, are you?' she asked, again and again, judgment in her voice."

We're angry at the people who died for the way they were with us before they died.

"In my father's eulogy," says Ted, "the minister talked about 'the blessed hope' that we would see our 'beloved husband and father' again. *Hell, no,* I thought. *Beloved? Don't make me laugh. He incested me, 'the beloved.' He beat my mother, 'the beloved.'*

"I never want to see you again, you no-good, hypocritical *beloved.*"

How quickly even the pink and blue memories of a birth day are wrapped in bitter black.

If you don't think you're angry as a griever, check yourself out.

• Are you unduly disgruntled with the annoyances of everyday life? Perhaps you've displaced your grief-anger onto Sally who slights you, or Dr. Hughes who humiliates you, or just the normal "hogging" tendencies of those with whom you live.

• Are you depressed? I encouraged myself to cry a few days ago when depression settled in, when I realized that it was depression. Strange how depression itself keeps you from recognizing that you are depressed. But crying didn't lift my depression until I also encouraged myself to be angry.

You cannot feel angry and not feel alive. You cannot feel angry and feel depressed. Unexpressed anger is the number one cause of depression.

• Are you sad? "Here," I say to clients, making a hollow with the palm of my hand, "this soft underbelly of your hand is your sadness." Then I turn my hand over and tap the hard arch of the top of my hand. "And this is your anger. Why are you sad? Because someone has hurt you. Why are you angry? Because someone has hurt you. If someone *pows* you, your instinct is to *pow* back."

You cannot be hurt and not feel both sad and angry. Look on *sad-angry* as one word.

• What happens when you exaggerate the anger you don't think is there? Practice saying, "Blast you for not being there when I needed you!" to someone who wasn't there when you needed them. Spit the words out with venom, even if you consciously feel no venom, and watch for churning within.

• Check out the places in your body where you store your anger. How tense are your shoulders? How active your ulcer? How frequent your headaches?

• What changes in mood do you experience when the anniversary of your *love's* death draws near?

Several years after Peggie died, Joe and I both became irritable early in June, couldn't say a decent word to each other. Couldn't figure out why till it dawned on us that June 6th was coming up—June 6th—the day Peg died.

It's called Anniversary Reaction, a recognized phenomenon in the mental health field. We grievers *know*; on some level of consciousness we *know* when our *love's* death day is drawing near. How the sad-angry memories of a death day rip through us on the anniversary of that day. How morose, how edgy, how rageful we become.

How quickly even the pink and blue memories of a *birth day* are wrapped in bitter black.

I imagined her sitting in an empty chair and yelled my lungs out at her.

So . . . once you realize how much anger you have inside you, how do you let it out?

One way is by confronting the person with whom you're angry.

I feel no anger toward anyone in the hospital connected with Peggie's death. She lived a long life for someone with as severe C.F. involvement as she had. But Joey died when he was twelve—such a little forty-five-pound boy—and he died because of the neglect of someone in the hospital, someone I'll call Mrs. Rollins.

"Confront her," my therapist said when I told him the story. "It will help you get rid of your anger, and think what it will do for Mrs. Rollins to say she's sorry. She must know what she did."

I didn't confront her in person, nor is it always best to confront the person with whom you are angry directly, though usually it is. I didn't have the courage to do so. I didn't think Mrs. Rollins would admit to her error for fear of legal action. She had, in fact, before I'd left the hospital—without my Joey—told me that something I had done was responsible for his death.

But I did confront her in my mind. I imagined her sitting in front of me in an empty chair and yelled my lungs out at her—yelled my lungs out at her again and again when I felt angry at her again, and again.

"I seethed with rage when Craig left," says Jan, "twenty-six hours a day. Accusing. Judging. Sentencing. I poured it out in my journal. I rattled on with friends on the phone. I cursed. Used every vulgarity. I poured it out in letters to Craig, letters I didn't mail. Wished every conceivable abuse upon him.

"How dare he let someone else step into the life that belonged to me, take my name, my future—and that someone my best friend, and Carrie's school teacher? How dare he destroy Carrie's trust in men, her interest in education?

"I'm not basically a physical person. I'm not a person who can just process interiorly. I'm a verbal person. I walked in the woods and vomited my rage out in words."

"Every time I drive past the old house," says Gracie, "I imagine myself uprooting that scrawling birch the new people planted out front, and if it's rained recently, I turf their lawn."

Mmmm . . . are uprooting and turfing forms of confrontation? What do you think?

Sometimes I sit Mrs. Rollins in a chair and confront her in a kind, caring way, but I still tell her how I feel about what she did. Confronting is not synonymous with maiming or destroying. Anger is not synonymous with aggression. I have no desire to harm Mrs. Rollins, nor did Jan at-

The Toughest Days of Grief

tack Craig in person, nor did Gracie in fact damage the lawn of her old house.

I do not want to say anything in this book to reinforce patterns of hostility in grievers who are habitually or dangerously hostile. More anger can be bad for their health. Heart attacks strike with above-average frequency. Other people back away.

But we're not talking about chronic anger here.

I emphasize confrontation in this chapter especially for church people, who often associate any expression of anger with sin and so deal with anger by repressing it, often under the *guise* of forgiveness.

Of course, this is a book about special occasions. Should we confront the objects of our rage at a birthday party or a bridal shower? People make special efforts to be nice on special occasions.

Well, express your anger with care whenever you express it, and, yes, exercise special wisdom and restraint on special days. Confront your nemesis in an empty chair, or confront an uninvolved person as a stand-in, but know that anger rises when anger rises. Move with the tide.

I found some pictures of Joey and Peggie the other day, but I cried too hard to look at them.

Another way to release your anger is by understanding why the people you're angry at acted the way they did.

When Joe's family arrived for Joey's funeral, his father held forth in our living room for two hours on the rights of minority groups in the Fiji Islands. I all-but-fainted.

And then it was picture-taking time. "No, Meg, you and Peg step out of the way. This is just for original Woodsons. Who knows when we'll have another family reunion?"

Oh, so that's what this is—a family reunion? Did you see the look on Peg's face when you asked her to step out of the *family*?

The next day Joe's family, and mine, too, took off for a joy ride up the Cuyahoga River. I curled up head-to-knees on a corner of my study floor while they were gone—a slanted, crazy-house floor.

But then, recently, my father-in-law said, in his quivering old-man voice, "I found some pictures of Joey and Peggie the other day, but I cried too hard to look at them."

It was the first time I knew that he cared. I understand now that at the time they all cared so much, they couldn't feel their feelings, had to make the days surrounding Joey's funeral like any other happy days. Maybe they had to preserve in pictures the family that was whole in order to survive their half-knowledge of the family that was *broken*.

I understand, too, that my passivity contributed to the way they were. I didn't ask for what I needed, and when I was around them, I acted happy, too. I didn't know much about grief back then either.

Was Brian's hugging other women about you, Maryanne? What else could his "acting like a jerk" have been about? I know you're hurting, but that's all the more reason to try to be objective.

People who feel able to cope with life's cruelest blows needn't be as angry at those who inflict the blows.

Yet another way to deal with your anger—especially excessive anger—is by understanding why you get as angry as you do. Generally people who like themselves are not as offended by people who criticize or reject them as people who do not like themselves.

People who see themselves as strong, able to cope with life's cruelest blows, needn't be as angry at those who inflict the blows as those who see themselves as unable to cope.

In his book, *Make Anger Your Ally*, Neil Clark Warren deals at length with the relationship between anger and low self-esteem. I recommend this book to all grievers who have a problem expressing anger.

Since women often have more of a problem expressing anger than men, I also recommend Harriet Goldhor Lerner's book, *The Dance of Anger: A Woman's Guide to Changing the Patterns of Intimate Relationships*.

Confronting those who add to our grief, understanding why they act the way they do, and why we get as angry at them as we do are three roads we grievers walk down to reach *undisguised* forgiveness.

Right now we're hiking the Appalachian Trail, 2100 miles from Georgia to Maine.

A last way to release your anger is through exercise. Rick and Raylene, members of my church, picked up the phone one Cleveland night and listened to a sheriff's voice tell them that the explosion of a small plane had illuminated the black Georgia sky that night, incinerating their only daughter and their only son.

"As time passed we found ourselves spending hours on the golf course," say Rick and Raylene, "and jogging and entering running events. We get our anger out in physical exertion. Right now we're hiking the Appalachian Trail, 2100 miles from Georgia to Maine."

Jog an extra mile on your angriest days, my fellow-grievers. Work out.

Getting our anger out can save our grief-ful lives.

So . . . after you've become aware of your anger and investigated ways to release it, what good can releasing your anger do?

• "I'd be so full of air, I'd think I'd explode. Getting my rage out relaxed me. My anger was so aggressive that if I hadn't imagined attacking that tree and that lawn, I could have attacked those people." — Gracie

• "I kept on ranting till I didn't need to hear myself anymore. When I spoke it, I understood it. When I vented it on paper, I could go back and retrieve it. And when, after two years, I did retrieve it, what unimportant stuff it was. I'd forgotten the things I'd obsessed on.

"My sister's husband left her ten years ago and moved to Arizona. Her son graduated from college this year in Phoenix, but my sister refused to go because she had vowed never to set foot in the state of Arizona. She never vented her anger; her anger is still her whole life.

"When Carrie gets upset because her friends' fathers take them places and Craig shows little interest in her, I still get angry, but the tail doesn't wag the dog. The anger is a compartment of my life now." —Jan

• "Anger enabled me to tolerate and bear and move past injustice, to let go of the illusion that somehow a debt was owed. What went wrong was not all Craig's fault." —Jan

• "Anger kept me from believing that what went wrong was all my fault, forced me to share the responsibility. I was not a devil. I was not a saint." — Jan

• "Being that angry at my father's funeral enabled me to *know* that his abuse was about him and not about me." — Ted

• "I lost my spine when Mark died. My anger found it for me again, gave me energy, got me a job, put me in school. Without anger I would have been paralyzed.

"And when my best friend turned out to be a fair-weather friend, anger gave me the push I needed to push her aside." — Maryanne

• "The lonely emptiness of our grief would have driven us mad were it not tempered by the release of pent-up anger. Our anger encouraged us to sweat two disturbed bodies into submission." — Rick and Raylene

• "The Christmas after Peggie died, Joe's Florida sister invited Joe and me to spend Christmas with her family. Joe's Texas sister and her husband were there, too.

"What a tender, broken-up Christmas it was for Joe and me, our first without either of our children. We took a walk one gentle, pine-scented Florida night and looked back at the house, light glowing from every window, illuminating the people inside.

"And I thought, *It's a home, with family in it, and I'm a part of it.* Remembering that lighted moment all those years long ago *crumbles* me still.

"And I'm glad I didn't write off Joe's family when Joey died, all those years longer ago yet.

"When Joey died, the loss of love left me feeling unlovable, so vulnerable, every slight registered as basic insult. I couldn't help losing my dead. Feeling my anger, and then letting go of it—I had to feel it before I could let go of it —kept me from losing my living, too." — Meg

Getting our anger out can save our *grief-ful* lives.

Yes, sometimes when we get angry, we look ugly, sound ugly, lose control. So, is losing control the end of the world?

Why not work at being angry and staying in control?

"Sometimes," says Maryanne, "my anger gets inappropriate, turns into hate."

Well, anger can harden into hate, and, of course, you want to control the hate. But anger is a normal healthy emotion, and using every excuse under the sun not to express it is abnormal and unhealthy.

Listen to Christ shout His invectives at those who abused others.

But anger is the opposite of forgiveness, you say. It's not the Christian way. This conviction dies hard.

But listen to Christ shout His invectives at those who abused others:

> Woe to you . . . you hypocrites! You travel over land and sea to win a single convert, and when he becomes one, you make him twice as much a son of hell as you are. . . . Woe to you . . . you hypocrites! You are like whitewashed tombs, which look beautiful on the outside but on the inside are full of dead men's bones and everything unclean. . . . You snakes! You brood of vipers! — Matthew 23:15-33

And then listen to Him weep over these same people *after His tirade*:

> O Jerusalem, Jerusalem . . . how often I have longed to gather your children together, as a hen gathers her chicks under her wings. — Matthew 23:37

The sin of the church today is not lack of forgiveness but premature forgiveness. Anger is the road we travel to get to forgiveness. We Christians, trying to be like the fictitious "meek and mild" Christ, become make-believe people.

There is little we can do in this world that is more Christian than using the energizing force of our anger to respond in a positive way to our hurt, to move out and do good in the world. Little catapults us into action like anger.

Martin Luther said, "When I am angry I can write, pray, and preach well, for then my whole temperament is quickened, my understanding sharpened, and all mundane vexations and temptations gone."

Anger in the Bible, says Warren, is most often associated with aggression, and biblical prohibitions against anger must be viewed in that light. "God," he says, "is reported as being angry several hundred times in the Old Testament alone. Jesus was regularly angry in relation to those who opposed him and toward his own disciples."

I asked Maryanne how she had expressed anger as a child and what happened to her when she did. "I laid on the floor and kicked and held my breath," she said, "till my father threw cold water on me."

Most parents throw cold water on their children's anger.

"But I did have Gamma," says Maryanne. "Gamma held me on her lap and I'd talk and cry my anger out with her. Gamma loved me no matter what I did. Gamma *saved my soul*."

If church or home have taught you to bottle up your anger, find a Gamma who will shout encouragement to you as you learn to unbottle it.

Anger is tricky. What better way to take control of your life as a griever than by taking control of your anger?

So, what change for the better will expressing your grief-anger bring about for you? For others? Should you express your anger in ways that are comfortable for you? Or uncomfortable? Is your tendency to sit on your anger? To use it to mistreat others? What is your growing edge where anger is concerned?

"Only the weak are afraid of emotion." Not the meek, the weak.

Get mad.

Plan Ahead:

In the week preceding your wedding anniversary, search out a selection of magnets that reveal who your *love* was to you—and is to you no more. When *the day* arrives, arrange the magnets on your refrigerator and feel the specific sadness and anger they elicit.

Hold a pillow and pummel it on Mother's Day. Talk to the person responsible for *her* death. . . . Now hug the pillow and see if you are ready to forgive.

Use what would have been your *love's* graduation day as a day of decision. Put your anger into working for a cause, perhaps a cure for the disease that killed *him*. Or join MADD. Or SADD.

Develop a cleansing ritual to be carried out at night when you can't sleep, before or after any special day: play a tumultuous piece of music on the piano; *attack* your messiest closet; be reckless—stay in the shower till all the hot water runs out.*

Welcome *your child*—you as a child—into your arms again. Encourage *her* to remember a time in her childhood when she was not permitted to be angry and give her permission to express that anger now.*

---

* Indicates suggestions appropriate for those bereaved by divorce as well as death.

CHAPTER 6

. . . .

Guilty Days

. . . .

"Hast thou seen the wounds?" said Michael,
"Knowest thou thy sin?"
"It is evening, evening," sang the blackbird
"Let her in! Let her in!"

"Yes I have seen the wounds,
And I know my sin."
"She knows it well, well, well," sang the blackbird,
"Let her in! Let her in!"
From "Glastonbury" by Henry Kingsley

. . . .

*I*n her book *Hatter Fox*, Marilyn Harris tells the story of Hatter, a young Indian woman full of her carefree ways, and Teague Summer, a white doctor determined to fit Hatter into civilized society. How they aggravated *and reverenced* one another.

As the book closes, Hatter meets Summer in the town square to help her deposit her first paycheck in the bank, but she chatters about a picnic in the mountains the next day. She doesn't have the check.

"It was just a piece of paper, Summer."

"Don't be stupid, Hatter. . . . You are going to go right back to the store, and you are not going to come back until you find that check."

"What about tomorrow?"

"Forget tomorrow." Hatter came running back waving the small white piece of paper in her hand. She didn't see the tour bus . . . Later Summer learned he had attacked the tour bus, that it had taken several men to pull him away "from the senseless task of pummeling steel."

> I could not admit for a while that I knew the truth, that she was dead, that I was responsible. . . . All I knew was that there was no escape. Anywhere. . . .
>
> No affection, no loyalty, no compassion, no tie is as strong and abiding with a living person as it is with a dead one. We must learn to live with our last words, our final actions, our sins of omission and commission, our neglects and regrets . . . because there will be nothing else. . . .
>
> I know that I must make a new beginning. But something has been permanently destroyed in me. . . . I feel an overwhelming sadness when confronted deep in myself with the fact that I could do nothing except kill her. . . .
>
> Something is wrong in me and the world, and I don't know how to fix it . . . this lack, this surplus, this something that is wrong in me and the world.

Guilt kills our belief in the trueness of our love, in the meaning of our lives.

We grievers can live with the death of a *love* if we must, but we cannot think that we might be *their killers*. We cannot think that we did not do everything for them—at the end—that we could do. We cannot think that we were not—at middle or the beginning—the friend or the lover he or she wanted us to be.

Guilt kills our belief in the *trueness* of our love, in the meaning of our lives.

Guilt kills surviving relationships. Unable to live with our guilt, or what seems our guilt, we project it onto those around us.

"I don't care what diagram the doctor draws to show the gene coming from both parents," the father of a child dead from sickle-cell anemia screams at his wife. "*You* produced this child."

Disease or accident killed our *loves*. Guilt kills our souls.

"Does everyone know," asks Summer, "that when they die, we die?"

And on what days do we grievers feel more this *dead way*—this dreadful, guilty way—than on the days that commemorate our special relationship with our *love*?

On what day do bereaved parents or bereaved children feel more guilty than on Mother's Day or Father's Day, days that extol the perfect parent, who deserves the perfect child? What day elicits more impossible expectations for bereaved spouses of what their marriages should have been than their wedding anniversaries?

And, ah, our *love's* death day, the day that marks the end of all our chances to atone. For those of us grievers subject to guilt, every special day calls forth its special brand of grief-guilt.

As guilt-ridden as I am, the fact that some grievers are not guilt-ridden astounds me.

However, while all grievers feel sadness and anger, not all grievers feel guilt.

"I don't feel any guilt for my divorce," says Jan. "I loved Craig unconditionally. Even he knew that. 'You should never have loved asking nothing in return,' he told me. 'It made you a sap.'"

Not all grievers feel appreciable guilt.

"I feel a little guilt that Mark's dead and I'm alive," says Maryanne, "but that's all the guilt I feel. I'm so much older. I would have gladly traded places with him."

"I said a couple things to my mother when I was taking care of her before she died I wish I hadn't said," a friend tells me, "but I don't *need* to dwell on such things the way you do."

As guilt-ridden as I am, the fact that some grievers are not guilt-ridden astounds me.

Of course, some grievers feel guilty and don't know it.

"I don't feel any guilt around my mother's death," says Gracie.

"I remember when Joe's mother died," I told her, "how we raced from Cleveland to Memphis to get there in time, and we did. We each had a private moment to say goodbye to her.

"Then we had lunch with old friends, and we stayed and stayed, talking and laughing, and I was beside myself that Mother Woodson would die while we were gone, and she did."

"But Joe felt no guilt. 'I said what I wanted to say to her, Meg.'

"Now she wasn't my mother, and we would have gotten back in time had Joe heeded my nagging, but I felt awesome guilt.

"No one should die alone, Gracie." I said it with feeling, and it nudged to her conscious mind feelings of guilt even plain-spirited, open-faced Gracie had pushed into her subconscious.

"My mother had surgery when I was fifteen, Meg. I visited her in the hospital on Christmas Day, and she was doing fine. 'I'm not coming tomorrow,' I told her. 'Lucy and I are gonna show each other our presents tomorrow.' Then the next day while I was with my friend, my mother died.

"Funny, all that happened fifty years ago, but it's as clear as if it happened yesterday. You know, now that I think of it, every Christmas I feel real bad."

It may be that your guilt, like Summer's, is so painful you "cannot admit to it." Or you can find "no words anywhere to name it."

It doesn't matter at the beginning whether your guilt is justified or exaggerated or altogether imagined; it only matters that you feel it.

Logic don't dispatch that cat. Not at first.

"I know we want our clients to feel their sadness and anger," Monica, a counselor friend, told me recently, "but guilt is such a yukky feeling. We don't want our clients to feel yukky."

Even professionals forget that if you want to get over any feeling, first you must feel it—speak it out in front of another—feel it out in front of someone other.

Guilt: "remorseful awareness of having done something wrong." —*American Heritage Dictionary*

"Once, Monica, I told Joey how much his being satisfied with me just as I was meant to me, and he said, 'Yeah, Mom, but I just wish you weren't always so busy.'

"And that's the one thing that registers with me—his one criticism. I *was* always busy. I regret that so. I knew I wouldn't always have Joey. I should have been perfect for him."

I didn't know I'd ever thought that until I said it out loud to Monica, and then I knew I'd always thought that. But as soon as I *said that*, I knew how silly the thought was. As soon as I *felt that*, I began *not to feel that*.

The black, sinuous substance of guilt sneaks up on us with animal cunning. It settles its pulsing flesh upon us and hisses and spits and tears.

Logic don't dispatch that cat. Not at first. First we join with the cat, know its weight, know its claws. First we *catch that cat*.

The Toughest Days of Grief

Look our guilt right in its gleaming green eyes: *If only I had . . . If only I could undo . . .* Exaggerate our guilt: *My guilt can never be erased because . . . No one else has ever done anything as . . .*

They're such tear-stained things, the pages of our guilt.

"Joey got the measles, Monica, and then he was in the hospital with a viral infection in his lungs. Usually he was up and about in the hospital, but this time he stayed in bed even when the infection cleared up, didn't read his Hardy Boys book, didn't work on his Frankenstein model.

"The nurses said it was because he'd been in the hospital so long. I should have realized that wasn't it. 'Take him home,' the nurses said. 'Take him home,' the doctor said. I should have argued with the doctor.

"But I didn't, and the next time Joe left to visit Joey, I asked him to bring Joey home. And when Joe called from the hospital and said, 'If you could see how he is, Meg, you wouldn't ask me to bring him home,' I exploded.

"'Oh, Joe, everybody says to bring him home. Bring him home.'

"'It goes against everything in me, Meg. If you could just see him.'

"'I've been making trips across town to see him for six weeks, Joe. I don't have one more trip in me. JUST BRING JOEY HOME.'"

So he did, and two days later Joey's heart failed, and by the time we got him back to the hospital everything—his heart, his lungs, his kidneys—everything was closing down.

BRING JOEY HOME. If only I hadn't said it. BRING JOEY HOME. How could I have said it?

I sobbed as I told Monica the story. I've sobbed all day as I've relived it.

Guilt: "a painful feeling of self-reproach resulting from a belief that one has done something wrong or immoral." —*New World Dictionary*

We don't always think of guilt as being painful, but it is painful.

Tears are an appropriate response to guilt as well as to sorrow. There's so much sorrow in guilt. So much pain. So much self-reproach that we did what we did or didn't do what we didn't do—and that what happened as a result happened.

Peggie introduced me to *Hatter Fox* a few months before she died. "I want you to read this book, Mother, and see if you cry on the same pages I cried on."

I did, on the guilt pages. They're such tear-stained things, the pages of our guilt.

Guilt is the yukkiest, thickest, most pervasive, *saddest* feeling in the world, and the second thing we can do with it is the same thing we do with any sadness—cry it out.

I shrank in my pew waiting for catastrophe to strike.

"Do you feel any guilt connected with the children's deaths, Joe?"

"No. I always tried to look ahead, do what I could all the way along so when the time came, I wouldn't feel guilty."

"Come on, Joe. No father's perfect. You must feel some guilt."

He laughed. "Only the guilt that comes from being a part of the human race."

Joe wasn't *cursed*. Truly *not cursed*. How light he must feel. I'd float away up in the sky were I *not cursed*.

"You weren't made to feel guilty in your home when you were growing up, Joe?"

"No. Stupid, yes. Guilty, no."

"You didn't feel guilty because you were stupid?"

"No. Just stupid."

That's what my exaggerated guilt went back to, of course: a home in which "What's wrong with you?" was the refrain. A home in which I was made to feel responsible for my mother's happiness, for her very life.

How easy then, as an adult, to believe that I was to blame for producing children with something wrong with them—and to believe that somehow I should have been able to keep them from dying.

And then the church in which I grew up shouted at me how bad I was. Week after week. They said that everyone was guilty, but they made me feel that I alone was guilty— of every sin. God's punishment was sure. I shrank in my pew waiting for catastrophe to strike.

And when it did—I knew my sins had found me out.

"I feel the full weight of defeat," says Summer of Hatter's death. Defeat? Yes, a word you expect from Summer when you know that earlier the book says he was accustomed to defeat, accustomed to "the always slightly disappointed expression in parental eyes."

So . . . did the church or home in which you grew up instill guilt in you? Who in particular did this? Was blame yelled into you? Beaten into you? What were the litanies of disapproval?

Was the fun poked at you really about you, or was it about the person who did the laughing and the pointing? How much of what you were shamed for was just the immaturity of childhood? How much condemnation did you deserve?

A third thing you can do with your guilt is to recognize the source of your guilt-proneness. Nothing distances you from the effects of guilt-instilled like recognizing how and why it was instilled, venting anger at—and then forgiving—the instiller.

So you alone were responsible for Joey's death?

When I finished choking out my BRING JOEY HOME story to Monica, she said, "So you alone were responsible for Joey's death?"

"Well, maybe the doctors and nurses, too. But I was Joey's mother. I knew him better than anyone else."

"And you had more medical expertise?"

"No, Monica, I didn't have more medical expertise." How obvious, but how hard to say. Yet, once I said it—the first rational thing I said about my guilt—I was on a roll.

"And, come to think of it, Joe didn't *have* to bring Joey home because I said to.

"We always knew the measles could kill our children. We traveled fourteen hundred miles to get them vaccinated when the measles vaccine first came out. We were responsible parents. So what about the irresponsible people who put out the early vaccine and didn't notify us that it wasn't always effective?

"And what about the mother of the boy who gave Joey the measles, the irresponsible mother who never got her son vaccinated?"

When I say I was on a roll, I don't mean that rationality came easily, but that with effort I could make it come.

And as I thought objectively about these others who, with me, shared responsibility for Joey's death, the weight of sole responsibility slipped away. I hadn't known how heavy a load it was till I began—just began—to feel light.

A fourth thing you can do with your guilt is to force yourself to think logically about it. It's scary, I know. We're afraid of where logic will lead us. But it's not only the feelings we hide from that destroy us; it's the facts we hide from as well.

Yet I was used to my guilt. BRING JOEY HOME. I hung on to my guilt. BRING JOEY HOME. I had to live with those last words, BRING JOEY HOME. I was bound to my son by my last words, my final actions . . .

"Why just your last words?" asked Monica.

Why indeed?

"Oh, Monica, had I been back then the person I am now, I'd have raised a ruckus. SOMETHING IS WRONG, AND I WON'T BRING JOEY HOME TILL YOU FIND OUT WHAT'S WRONG."

"It sounds like you did the best you could do as the person you were at the time, Meg."

"Maybe, but my best wasn't good enough."

Still, I've worked hard at changing myself. Feeling proud of the assertive person I am now makes it easier for me to look logically and forgivingly at the nonassertive person I was then.

How can I blame myself for having done the best I could?

Don't you make comments sometimes you don't mean?

I must have done some things right with my children, otherwise how could Peggie have dealt with her guilt the way she did after Joey died? I kept notes on how she did it:

> "I sure was awful to Joey," she admitted. "Ya know how he would have one week to pick television programs and I would have the next? Well, I used to figure way ahead to when there would be a vacation week and count back and fix it so I'd get to pick then. I was terrible to him. . . . *Just like a regular sister.*
>
> "And when we were in the hospital together the time before last, and the nurses made Joey walk up and down the hall seven times? I mean, nobody would listen when he said how tired he was. And he came in my room in that

itty-bitty wheelchair all exhausted and tried to tell me about it, and I yelled at him to get out.... *Of course, I didn't know he was dying.*

   "And we had good times together, too. Like when we built the house for Teddy on one of the shelves of Joey's bookcase, and we cut the rug for the floor and glued the watch to the ceiling for a clock and all?

   "Remember how he used to wire his room so if you guys opened the door his alarm clock went off? Well, I helped with that. *I know I bossed him a lot, but when he was doin' stuff in his room, he bossed me, too."*

If Peggie felt any prolonged guilt, it was because she didn't grieve as Joe and I grieved.

   "I keep waiting for it to hit me the way it has you guys, but it never does."

   "We both got our ears pierced six months ago, right, Peg?" I said. "Look at your ears. You can hardly see where they were pierced. Now look at my gaping holes. Young people mend more quickly than older people. Be glad you're young."

   Peggie scrutinized my ear lobes. "How gross. You can see the light clear through. And your ears are still gooey. Are your ears always going to be gooey?

   "Now for goodness' sakes, Mother, I don't know what you're cryin' about this time, but if it's because you're still bound and determined that you weren't a good enough mother to Joey, instead of moanin' and groanin' about it, *why not just decide to do a better job on me?*

"You don't believe me when I make my comments about your not bein' a good mother, do you? *Don't you make comments sometimes you don't mean?*"

I'm sick of listening to myself: BRING JOEY HOME. *My best wasn't good enough.* I'm ready to listen to my daughter. I tell you, I'm tired of my self-hate.

Yes, I'm human. I make mistakes. And some of my mistakes have been life and death mistakes. I wish it weren't so, but it is so. So much of my admission of guilt in the past has been an attempt to deny guilt. It feels good to feel guilt's weight, guilt's claws.

"I did it. I contributed to Joey's death." There, I've said it—and it hasn't destroyed me. "I did it." It feels good to say it.

And I'll tell you something else; at times, when they were alive, I resented my children. Every day it was therapy on one. Therapy on the other. Fix their aerosols. Count out their pills. Sterilize their mist tents.

But I did those things. Yes, I did some things wrong, but I did some things right, too.

What about the long talks Peg and I had together? What about the wisdom I instilled? What about the courage in me she picked up on and made her own? Who nurtured in Peggie the self-esteem that enabled her to handle her guilt so magnificently?

Me. I did. Her father and I did.

No, I wasn't the perfect mother. But I wasn't a monster-mother either. Mature people seek out middle ground.

Was Peggie a perfect child? Joey a perfect son?

Grow up, Meg.

Summer was wrong when he said he "could do nothing but kill" Hatter. The first time he saw her, in a jail cell, she slid a knife in his back. When he got out of the hospital, he followed her to the State Reformatory and got her out of the cage.

Did you push Hatter in front of the bus, Summer? Think, Summer, think. Did you do your best to train her to look both ways before crossing any street in her life?

Summer has to retrain his mind. Make himself spend fifteen minutes every day thinking of the good he did Hatter. Maybe an hour a day to begin with. It's no small job we guilt-prone grievers have ahead of us.

If I had not been with my children at the moment of their deaths, while I would feel enormous sadness, at this point I would not feel guilt. Even family members have to eat. Sleep. Occasionally we have to get out of the room just because we have to.

Yes, something is wrong in me "and everyone in the world," and there is no quick fix for this need, this surplus in me and everyone in the world. But unlike Summer I don't take this as condemnation; I take this as comfort. I could not be the Mother's Day mother I tried so hard to be.

The rotten mothers of the world don't feel the most guilt. Good mothers feel the most guilt.

***Something has not been permanently destroyed in you.
You will not let it be.***

"I felt no guilt over my divorce," says Jan, "but I did over Bobby, my baby boy. I refused to look at him, didn't want to be responsible for his care. He only had half a heart—and so did I.

"'Do you want to hold him?' the nurses asked. I bolted, ran to the bathroom and heaved and sobbed. He was slit from his little neck to his groin, hooked up to IV, heart monitor. *Die, die*, I wept. *If you're going to die, die.*

"Then I saw myself in the mirror as he must see me. It crushed me, and I went to him and held him and loved him. He shouldn't have lived as long as he did. I thought it was because I held him.

"I got a virus the week before he died and couldn't visit him. I thought it was because I didn't hold him.

"I feel no judgment of mothers who walk away from their babies. It's all they can do."

"I used to shop lift," Jan went on—a colorful figure, our Jan. "I never felt a twinge of guilt. I needed the things I took. Craig wouldn't pay for them. The stores wouldn't miss them. But the minute Bobby died, an endless clothesline stretched before my eyes hung with slips and sheets I had taken, and earrings and Carrie's dresses . . ."

And so this chapter closes with an unfinished sentence. I hope I'm not giving you simplistic formulas in this book, slippery hand-holds to grasp as you struggle to keep your footing in churning waters.

Living is not easy. Or dying. Or grieving. And especially the guilt part of grieving is not easy.

Yes, my memories of my children will always burn as well as bless, but I want the blessing part now.

And blessings on you, my fellow-griever. Something has not been permanently destroyed in you. You will not let it be.

> "*Thou bringest no offerings,*" *said Michael,*
> "*Nought save sin.*"
> *And the blackbird sang, "She is sorry, sorry, sorry.*
> *Let her in! Let her in!*"

Let yourself in.

Plan Ahead:

Ask someone to role-play your mother in heaven on Mother's Day. Tell her the things you're most sorry for and see how she responds. How has her new environment changed her?

Sit in your father's chair at the table on Father's Day. Get inside your father's skin as you look around at the members of the family. What does your father have to be sorry for? What should he regret as he looks at you?

Hold your inner child tight on Grandparent's Day. Remind *him* of ways his grandparents bragged about him, and then you praise him, praise him, praise him.*

Use your *love's* death day or the day of your divorce to make a list of the ways you failed *her*—and then burn the list.*

Tack this quotation on the sun visor in your car: "Beware of the man who does not forgive himself. It's ungodly." —John Ehle, *The Road* *

---

* Indicates suggestions appropriate for those bereaved by divorce as well as death.

The Toughest Days of Grief

CHAPTER 7

∙ ∙

Your First Days Back in Church

∙ ∙

I thought I heard Him calling! Did you hear
a sound? A little sound!

James Stephens

∙ ∙

I got to church early the first time I went back after my
husband died," a client tells me, "and then some teenagers
came in talking, and I leaped up, ran out of church, drove
ten miles to the Metropark, and watched the ducks. To
this day I don't know what got into me."

Well, I suspect that what got into this widow is that getting herself into the church building created so much
stress that the little noise the teenagers made created more
stress than she could handle, and she bolted. Sitting with
the ducks eased her distress.

I suspect, also, that what got into her gets into a lot of
us grievers the first time we go back to church, or the
second . . .

Why should our first time back to church cause us less pain than our other firsts?

Sue didn't go back to church for two months after Suzette's death. "I just couldn't," she sobs.

She goes now. "But it's so hard," she sobs. "Suzette always took the hymn books out of the pew racks and stacked them around my feet. Then when it was time for the children's sermon, instead of going up front, she stood in the aisle at the end of our pew and listened.

"I never get through the first hymn without crying, and when it's time for the children's sermon, I lose it altogether."

How could she not? Sue still drives to a town five miles away to avoid the supermarket where she pushed Suzette in the grocery cart. Week after week she describes for me her first trip to the post office without Suzette . . . her first time back to the dentist . . .

Why should our first time back to church cause us less pain than our other *firsts?*

"Suzette was baptized in our church," says Sue. "The people remember her from the beginning. I want them always to remember her. I could never go to another church. I could never go to our church and sit in another pew."

Perhaps it will help you stay in the church you went to with your *love*—if that's what you want to do—if you recognize the normality of the pain your memories bring you there.

For three years after Peggie's death I avoided driving past the hospital where she died. I avoided driving down the street you turn off to drive past the hospital.

The places that evoke deep feeling memories—sad or happy—are the hardest for us grievers to go back to.

So maybe we should *expect* going back to church to cause us more pain than our other *firsts*. Church, after all, is where our deepest feelings surface.

Not having anyone to hold the other half of the hymn book symbolizes their loss of their other half.

After his wife died, Jim, our elderly widower, had difficulty sitting in church with no one to share his hymn book. For many widows and widowers not having anyone to hold the other half of the hymn book symbolizes their loss of their other half.

"As soon as I began to be able to do things again," says Jim, "I joined the choir. There's a special camaraderie in the choir, and," he adds with a twinkle in his eye, "they can only afford sheet music for every two people."

"Al and I sat in the middle of the right side of the sanctuary," says Gracie. "After he died, I moved to the back pew on the left side. Ya know, *the widow's pew*. I don't feel so alone there.

"It's hard, though, and it's hard going home after church, too. *Somebody's gonna come*, I think, but nobody comes. I can't be too dependent on the kids. Other days there's stuff to do. I'm okay now eating out by myself on weekdays—nobody's gonna stare at me funny. But on Sundays you see families together. I go out to Sunday dinner with Alice or Yvonne now, ya know, from the widow's pew."

It may help you to sit smack in the pew you sat in with your Suzette, or it may help you to go to an earlier service or to join a new Sunday school class.

Yes, going back to church will cause you pain, but there are things you can do to lessen the pain somewhat.

What better place to cry and be comforted than in church?

Sometimes we grievers resist going back to church because we don't want to make a public display of our emotions.

"It used to be that when I was in church and the tears came, I found something to look up at on the ceiling," says Gracie, "bent my head way back to keep the tears in my eyes, but after a few months, my neck got stiff. I used to try to squelch the memories that came to me in church, but now I think, if I don't have my good memories, what do I have? And I let the tears roll down my cheeks."

Good for Gracie.

Jim took off his glasses, gold-rimmed, as he told me about the other half of the hymn book. "See how the metal is corroded on the inside," he said. "That's from the salt in my tears, many of which were shed in the back row of the choir."

Good for Gracie and Jim. Where should we be able to cry if not in church?

The memory of the blackened rims of Jim's glasses fills me with regret that I didn't find *a choir* to sit with in church when I needed to cry.

"The first time I went back to church, I cried at the time of the children's sermon," says Sue, "and everybody around me cried with me.

"The second time I went back to church and cried at the time of the children's sermon, I walked out," says Sue, "and everybody around me walked out with me."

Sometimes I get upset with the people in my congregation because I didn't get much comfort from them when either of my children died, but then I ask myself if I let them see that I needed comfort.

What better place to cry and be comforted than in church?

When we cut ourselves off from our deepest feelings, we cut ourselves off from the deepest feelings of the Loving One.

Yes, we melt at all our first-times-back, but we melt away at our first time back in church.

It has to do with our knowing, underneath all our doubting of God and our anger at Him, that He cares about us as no one else cares. That it's safe to cry with Him. That He is The Comforter.

"Oh, God, before whom all thoughts are known, all desires felt," intones the preacher, and God wraps His arms around us, and we know He knows where we are.

"And God shall wipe away all tears from their eyes, and there shall be no more pain," intones the preacher, and we wrap our arms around God. He knows where our loved ones are.

"Lord, have mercy. Christ, have mercy. Lord, have mercy." Yes, we will make it through the night.

It's hard for us grievers to go back to church because it's so ... holy. I cannot put the words into my computer without crying.

If we don't let ourselves cry in church, we not only cut ourselves off from our deepest feelings but also from the deepest feelings of The Loving One. From His deepest loving.

Ask your minister for what you need. He may not know. You may get it.

There are churches, however, that are not receptive to our tears.

On the last Sunday of Joey's life, I slipped out of the hospital and into the nearest church for morning worship. When we were invited to greet those around us, the woman next to me said, "Do you live in the area?"

"Right now I'm living in Babies and Children's Hospital with my son."

"Oh, but he's not very ill?"

"He's very ill," I choked.

"Oh, but he is going to get better?"

"No, he's not going to get better," I said and broke down altogether.

The woman pressed her questions—I didn't want to answer—yet the look on her face as I answered said, *How low class.* The people in that church were too sophisticated to handle personal announcements, let alone public displays.

One thing you can do if you go to such a church is to get what you can, not from the people, but from the service. Cry on the way home.

As I'd left the hospital for church that *last Sunday morning*, I breathed a prayer for reassurance that Joey would be with God when he died, that my son would continue to grow, to become.

The opening hymn was "Joyful, Joyful, We Adore Thee," sung to Beethoven's "Ode to Joy":

> *Joyful, joyful, we adore Thee,*
> *God of glory, Lord of love,*
> *Hearts unfold like flowers before Thee,*
> *Opening to the son above.*

We sang "Joyful, Joyful" as the opening hymn at Joey's funeral. "I've never heard our congregation sing like that," people said. We sang "Joyful, Joyful" again at Peggie's funeral.

I'd live with the disdain I got that Sunday morning to get to the strains of "Hearts unfold like flowers before thee" any day.

Another thing you might do as a griever in a non-feeling church is to try to change the church.

When Sue's minister visited her after Suzette's death, she wept out her sorrow before him; he talked about the church's building program. She asked him if he believed in an afterlife; he didn't answer. And on Sunday mornings, for all it cost Sue to sit in church, her memories stacked in tilting piles at her feet, what she got for a sermon was an intellectual discourse.

Sue spoke to her minister about her unmet heart-needs. Other members of the congregation expressed similar needs, and the minister changed.

"When he visits my husband and me now, he sits with us in our pain," says Sue. "He'll never be a hold-you-in-his-arms person, but nobody can believe how inspiring his sermons are."

Ask your minister for what you need. He may not know. You may get it.

I was always looking for something more.

If there's no way you can get what you need in your church, however, you may want to change churches.

"I was baptized Presbyterian," says Maryanne, "but I was always looking for something more. I got involved in astrology, in New Age, in Unity, but after Mark's death, none of it was enough. Then I tried the Episcopal Church, and I didn't have to believe Jesus loved me in the Eucharist, He just did.

"I get into my wounded child in church. Everything bad that's ever happened to me leaks out. When I kneel in the Episcopal Church, I can put my head on the pew in front of me and hide my face.

"My other way of communicating with God is in nature. One day when I was distraught over Mark, I went to Edgewater Park, to the top of the hill, climbed up on a picnic table and held myself. The wind blew off the lake, and I felt God's power. I looked at the bigness of the lake, and God was big, and I was a part of Him."

Be with God any way you can, my fellow-griever, but don't give up on the regularity and structure church gives to the feeding of your spirit unless you must. Don't give up on the company the church provides for your journey. Keep on finding ways to make church easier for yourself.

"Going back to church reminded us of the family joy we didn't have anymore," say Rick and Raylene. "The church was always related to family for us. It helped us to black out a lot of what went on in church and think about resurrection and reunion with the kids."

"I made up for what it cost me to go back to church by thinking of all it had given me," says Gracie. "Like way back when Joe made his first pastoral call on us. That was the first time anybody said I had worth."

If I can take losing my child, God can take my anger at Him.

Sometimes we grievers don't go back to church because we're angry at God. We don't want to be *where He is.*

"God was the scapegoat for two temporarily insane grievers," say Rick and Raylene. "We know now that we castigated Him undeservedly, but didn't Job do the same? Maybe Job set an example for what we're all supposed to do. God took our anger silently."

"I only know life's been sad as long as I can remember," says Jan. "The best man at my wedding killed himself. My father died—my father meant everything to me. My baby boy died. Craig's mother died—the first woman tender to me. My marriage ended. My mother died. I sent Larry away, the man I loved after Craig. He loved me, but he loved other women, too.

"Life isn't bearable as a crapshoot. I expected more from God than that. At what point is God accountable for the quality of life of His children? You're allowed to say what you really want when you pray, but that sure doesn't mean you'll get it.

"I don't have an enthusiasm for God right now. I have a hope. He's somebody the rest of you know and trust. Sometimes I decide to trust Him without knowing why.

My anger at God has settled into disappointment in Him, but if I express the disappointment, even that energizes me to move out of my sadness."

"It's as though my son were brutally tortured," says Maryanne, "murdered, and God watched and did nothing. If I were God, no child would die before a parent. If I can take losing my child, He can take my anger at Him.

"And not just because of Mark's pain—because of my pain. I had this sense that everything could and should be fixed, but God wouldn't fix my pain. Finally I said, 'I will process this grief or die from it,' and I knew the healing had to be a process and that I had to take authority over it, that it was a cooperative thing with God.

"First I had to feel enormous sadness that God had let this horror happen. Then I had to feel enormous anger. Then I could make a life."

God doesn't write us grievers out of His heart when we get angry at Him. No, our real anger at God leads us to a more real relationship with Him. How can we not get angry at God when He could have stopped someone we loved from dying—and didn't?

He has a funny way of loving us.

But what better place to express our anger at Him than *where He is.*

Our anger at God grows out of our love for Him. Don't we always get angriest at the people we love the most, whose love we trust the most? Whose love betrays us the most?

"Anything You want," Peg said to God of those last unspeakable weeks of her life. "Just make something bright and beautiful out of this for You."

And God said to Peg, *Let C.F. rip.* God said, *Let the unspeakable roll.*

Anger at God took me over after Peggie died, still does at times. Even now Joe and I feel alone in a world our children don't inhabit, and as we grow older, we feel scared.

Yet my anger at God encourages my love for Him to grow. It goes back to how we depress all feelings when we depress one feeling and release all feelings when we release one feeling we've depressed.

My anger at God breaks my love for Him into little pieces. I can feel it better when it's broken. I don't know why.

But I know I will not let my anger at God cut me off from my love affair with Him, will not let it keep me forever from our trysting place.

We think we do not want to be *where He is*—but we do.

Getting angry at God thrusts us into action. All anger energizes us, and anger at God is no exception. When we sit on our anger, we cannot move; when we light the fuse to the powder keg we're sitting on, we cannot not move.

We feel ugly when we're angry at God, just as we feel ugly when we're angry at people; but we also feel alive when we're angry at God, just as we feel alive when we're angry at people. And what more do we grievers want, aside from wanting our dead alive again, than to feel alive again ourselves?

A lot of our depression grows out of unexpressed anger at God.

We don't know who God is anymore. We don't know how to be with Him.

I remember Joe looking at a little picture of Joey after he died. I remember the lost, unbelieving shock in Joe's voice as he said, "Joey didn't get to grow up, did he, Meg?"

We'd been Abraham on the mountain offering our son to God in death if He wanted Him, but how we hoped He didn't want him, that He would give our son back to us as He had given Abraham's son back to him. We thought that protecting His people from tragedy was what He was about. We were wrong.

Sometimes we grievers stop going to church because we don't know who God is anymore. We don't know how to be with Him.

Did He cause this thing that happened to us? Or was this thing an accident? Why didn't He keep Jan's husband from leaving? Why didn't He keep Jim's wife from dying? Why didn't He keep my children from suffering? Why doesn't God do the things He doesn't do?

I got my first glimpse into my *response*—not answer, but *response*—to such questions sitting in second row, first seat, in Plain Geometry in high school.

"Parallel lines meet in infinity," said the teacher. "Yes, by definition parallel lines are equidistant at every point, yet we solve everyday geometric problems by using the theorem: Parallel lines come together in the farthest reaches of infinity."

How could this be?

I soon forgot where I sat in other classes, but I've never forgotten second row, first seat in Riemann Plain Geometry, where my young, know-it-all, scientific mind took its first step into the world of paradoxes, of unimaginable truth.

So when I began to wrestle with the question, "Why were my children born with cystic fibrosis?" second row-first seat was still with me.

Was their C.F. the result of an unlucky throw of genetic dice? Yes.

Did God control the throw of genetic dice? Yes.

Can I have it both ways? I can.

Was Peggie's long, painful death the result of a wonderfully strong-willed young woman refusing to die quickly or easily?

Is anything outside of God's will if we trust ourselves to Him?

I learned to lean heavily on whichever parallel line, whichever rail of the railroad track, moved me along best in my ride through life—my ride into the furthermost reaches of eternity where all comes together.

The rail of the track I leaned on heavily through all my children's cystic fibrosis was the Will of God rail. It helped me to believe that our family was living out God's plan for

The Toughest Days of Grief

us, that there was divine purpose in the seemingly cruel, uncharted course of our lives.

What got me through the days I lived in the hospital with Peg as she was dying was *Abandonment to Divine Providence*, a book by Jean-Pierre de Daussade, a seventeenth-century mystic. I carried it with me to the cafeteria, to the ladies' room, and a time or two I took *Divine Providence* to bed with me and slept with it at night.

Do you like my parallel-line theory? If so, you'll have to decide which side of the railroad track you need to shift your weight to at various times as you chug through the trials and the triumphs of your life.

There are gonna be times when no one else around is interested in helping you.

But one thing is bedrock for all of us at all the times of our lives: Nothing can happen to us, whatever the cause, that results in moving us outside God's love and care.

Why did God let this happen to me—if He loves me? we cry. It's the end of the question that does us in. The end of the question is always there, whether we verbalize it or not.

Feel the fear of that ending. Feel your way through the fear. We dare not live in a universe in which God is not love. Who is He if He is not love, and for whom is He love if not for each of us?

> *He heals the brokenhearted*
> *and binds up their wounds.*

The primary reason we grievers go to church is to rendezvous with God, who is love, especially now, especially for us.

The most special of your special days are the days you spend with Him.

"The thing that's helped me more than anything else since Al died," says Gracie, "along with faith in myself, is my faith in God. There are gonna be times when nobody else around is interested in helping you.

"You know what Frank Sinatra used to sing, 'You gotta have hope. If you don't, all you do is sit around and mope'?

"If I have hope in God *and* get up off my you-know-what, then I have courage to carry on."

You can bear the pain of your special days if you feel pleasure alongside the pain.

You can bear the pain of your special days if you feel the pain.

You can bear the pain of your special days if you feel it with people.

You can bear the pain of your special days if you feel it with Providence.

Yes, going back to church for the first time is a struggle. We cry and rage in church. We're afraid God won't be there. We're afraid God will be there. *Who is He?*

But nothing, my grieving friend, compares to feeling our pain with God's arms around us.

If you move into the center of your pain and stay there long enough, God will find you there. (author unknown)

Go, God.

Plan Ahead:

Make a list of your doubts about God. The first time you go back to church, go when there is no service. Sit alone in the sanctuary and read your list to God.*

The first time you go back to a church service, remember your *love* by putting flowers on the altar in *his* memory, or by giving a permanent gift to the church in *her* name: collection plates, cross, book for the library, chair for the church parlor.

Plan ahead where you will sit, with whom, what you will do if you cry, what you will do if the service becomes more than you can handle.*

Take the following quotations to church with you and meditate upon them in silence before the service begins:*

> Moreover, the truth that matters is not what we feel but the "fact" that God loves us whatever we feel, and His energies are always tending toward our health and well-being.
> —Leslie Weatherhead

> And Jesus said, "Come to the water, stand by my side.
> I know you are thirsty, you won't be denied.
> I felt every teardrop when in darkness you cried,
> And I strove to remind you that for those tears I died."
> —Marsha J. Stevens

> Blessed are those who mourn, for they will be comforted.
> —Jesus

---

* Indicates suggestions appropriate for those bereaved by divorce as well as death.

. . . .

CHAPTER 8

Thanksgiving

. . . .

For the gladness here when the sun is shining
at evening on the weeds at the river,
Our prayer of thanks.

Carl Sandburg

. . . .

*T*hanksgiving Day isn't a gift-giving day, but I have a gift for you anyway—a Thanksgiving story:

Pilgrims to Peggie's Place

Our Chevy was no *Mayflower,* and our *voyage* from Cleveland to Canton, Ohio, only seemed long that Thanksgiving Day, but Joe and I were weary, frightened, lost, and lonely pilgrims as we set out for Peggie's Place: a new world for us, an unknown and frightening world. How would we survive in Peggie's Place without our Peggie in it?

The day had a bleak, thankless look, the weeds along the wayside shaking their bowed beige heads at us as we passed, the dark brown soil in the fields beyond laid out in rectangles, the earth still in its furrows but hardened like . . . like the hardened rectangle of earth on a daughter's five-month-old grave.

Gray-brown trees silhouetted skeleton arms against a looming-gray sky, and the dampness of late November seeped into the car—and my bones—for I was on my way to say good-bye in a more final way than I'd yet done to the places Peggie had loved and to the Peggie I had loved and lost.

I'd settled down in the red and blue rocker in our Early American living room early that morning and forced myself to be thankful.

Thank you, God, that Peggie lived for twenty-three years.

Thank you, God, for the friend-times we had in her very own apartment-place.

And learned my first lessons of the day: one, that while once gratitude had bubbled spontaneously within me, now I had to force my simplest praise; and, two, that only such a fierce, determined habit of thanksgiving would get me through that fiercesome day.

Yet, thankful or not, we turned at every Canton Only sign with increasing dread, aware that only on our way to Peggie's Place had we made those turns before and that we would have no reason ever to make them again.

Then down from the highway I spied the gas station with the Bolin Oil sign overhead. How we'd laughed at that sign, Joe and Peg and I, over and over and over . . .

We left the highway at the Everhard-Whipple exit and headed into *Peggie's town*, drove down *Peggie's streets*. Joe parked in front of *Peggie's stores*, though they were closed for the holiday, all the stores where she and I had hunted for can openers and clocks and curtains. Usually when Peg had summoned me to Canton, it was to roam the stores with her.

Those vast empty parking lots enlarged my sense of desolation, especially at Sears where we'd unearthed so many of Peg's treasures, like the yellow drapes, a perfect match to her bright yellow bedroom walls. "The room will be a blaze of sunshine, Mother." And the butterfly towels, a perfect match to her bright flashing spirit.

"That was some *coincidence*, our coming here for drapes and finding the absolutely perfect ones on sale, right, *Ma*?" she asked, not believing that any happy coincidence in her life was not one of *God's incidents*.

"You don't think I'm spending too much money on myself, do you? I keep tellin' my friends they should ask me for anything they need." And then she'd had to find a place to rest and cough.

Sometimes now when the phone rang in Cleveland, just for a minute I thought, *Maybe it's Peg wanting me to come to Canton*. But sitting in those abandoned parking lots, I knew in the depths of my hollow heart I'd never saunter through Sears with my daughter again.

Oh, God, I'm not sure I can make it without her, but thank You, God, that she made it. Thank you for her courage and her cheeriness and her givingness and her faith.

And right then I learned my second lesson in thanksgiving: that I must give it at the end of my sentences. That I must not raise my thanks as prelude to despair:

Thank You, God, for all Peg's apartment meant to her, but Oh, God, all that work for nine months?

But raise my thanks as benediction on despair:

Oh, God, Peg only had her own place for nine months, but how much it meant to her. Thank You, God, that Peggie had her place at all.

And so, *Good-bye, Sears and Roebuck. Good-bye, waterbed store. I won't be seeing you again, but it was nice knowing you.*

And then Joe pulled in behind Canterbury Manors, and I clambered out of the car—I don't know how—and pulled open the building's heavy door. And there lay the brick Peggie'd found to hold the door open—a cement brick the only sign that this had once been Peggie Woodson's dwelling place.

I stumbled down the red-carpeted steps and stood in front of the door marked 10, remembering the times when love and joy had waited for me behind that door. "Well, how's my place coming, Mother? Have I overdone the rainbows? Will my friends feel the peace of God here? Is it a happy place for you, Mother?"

Oh, Peg, you will never open this door to me again, but: *Thank You, God, that You lived with Peggie here.*

I could have knocked on the door, explained who I was, but even if I'd been invited in . . . it wouldn't have been Peggie's Place. No, no, not ever again Peggie's Place.

The Toughest Days of Grief

And so I touched my fingers to my lips and then to the knob of the door marked 10—and wrenched myself away. Forevermore away from Peggie's Place.

Good-bye, No. 10 door. Good-bye, cement block, I sobbed and learned my final lesson of the day: that however I forced my thanksgiving or wherever I put it in my sentences, no amount of thanksgiving takes away the throes of living.

I felt ancient of days as we headed north on 77, ready to be gathered unto my children—Peggie, and Joey too, his body moldering under settled earth for nine years now.

I felt enamored of the weeping willows as we headed forevermore north from Peggie's Place. I wanted to crawl beneath the sad-gold branches of a willow. Wanted a storm to crash through the land, wanted to sway with the wind and shriek at nature gone savage, killing both my children. Wanted to raise my face to rivers of pain.

But even then, when the storm stilled, I would push out through the willow and say, *But I had them.*

Thank You, God. I had them.

Even then I would not curse God but bless Him forevermore in the aura of the weeping willow—and be blessed by my blessing of Him.

Yes, the air was still raw and the fields still barren as we drove north. Why had those Pilgrims proclaimed the first Thanksgiving Day in a season such as this? Of course, I knew the answer, but suddenly every bleached, brittle cornstalk guarding the roadside shouted to me of harvest reaped.

Oh, yes, I would lift my fallow heart in harvest song:

Thank You, God, for the Peggie-seed planted in the womb of my youth. Thank You, God, for Peggie's eager shooting forth into the day. Thank You for her first tender growth and for the sweet-heartedness of her everlasting youth. Thank You, God, for the accelerated ripening of her spirit till in her brief growing season her love of God and friend came to full fruit.

How I would miss her, but it was Thanksgiving Day and I gave thanks for Peggie-gathered-in.

It takes a lot of thanksgiving to make us truly thankful for our dead.

I wrote this story shortly after it took place. It took me a day and a half now to rewrite it. I'd forgotten how sore my grief was in the early months after Peggie died. I bent low in that new, heart-sore, unbelieving, unbelievable pain as I reexperienced it.

But I was unbelieving, too, at how crying out *Thank You, God, for this* and *Thank You, God, for that* over and over as I rewrote and rewrote tilted me up and stood me tall, on my feet.

Well, Thanksgiving Day is a day for giving thanks over and over: to repeat our thanks for the life our *loves* lived on earth; to reiterate our thanks for the life they live now in heaven; to recapitulate our thanks for all the good of all the years we lived with them and now live without them.

It takes a lot of thanksgiving to make us truly thankful for our dead.

Peg's illness made her more dependent on me than she wanted to be, kept her more the defiant adolescent than I wanted her to be. We had bad times, and when she died, it seemed in my guilt-prone soul that all our times had been bad.

But my thanksgiving and my thanksgiving and my thanksgiving left me knowing that we had good times, too. They feel like good times now.

And Peg's having a good time now, too. Unfortunately, society doesn't view heaven as exciting, if it catches sight of heaven at all. Doesn't view death as part-tragedy, which it is, but as all-tragedy, which it is not.

Yes, I believed that Peg was in *her own place* in heaven before I rewrote my story, *a place prepared for her*, but my thanksgiving and my thanksgiving and my thanksgiving offset society's unbelieving till I believed more fully and gave thanks more truly.

Glad thanks turns us glad.

It's easy on days in ordinary time to give thanks out of habit, but dutiful thanks doesn't turn us grievers around; no, glad thanks turns us glad.

Well, Thanksgiving is a holiday, by definition a happy day. It's easier to give thanks with gladness on Thanksgiving Day.

Thanksgiving is a family-and-friend holiday. It's easier to give thanks with gladness in the company of significant, smiling others. Even near-pagans among us bow their heads over the Thanksgiving turkey with ill-concealed grins of juicy anticipation.

Thanksgiving is a church holiday. It's easier to give thanks with gladness in the company of the church, the family of God—to sing our thanks, all the verses, with glad refrain:

> Come, ye thankful people, come,
> Join the song of harvest home.

Thanksgiving gets our praise down into the deep, good, black soil of our souls.

In his book *Lament for a Son*, Nicholas Wolterstorff says:

> The worst days now are holidays: Thanksgiving, Christmas, Easter, Pentecost, birthdays, weddings, January 31—days meant as festivals of happiness and joy now are days of tears. The gap is too great between day and heart. Days of routine I can manage; no songs are expected. But how am I to sing in this desolate land, when there's always one too few?

Yes, if it's our first Thanksgiving, or our second or third, with "one too few," we may resent song. It may do us good to warble a small, brown-sparrow note or two, but we may not be able or willing even to warble.

Most of us, however, are more than willing to talk about the ones we have lost, to trill their praise, and if that's all we can manage, that's all we should try to manage.

Every year since Peg died, Joe and I have had Thanksgiving dinner with one of her college professors and his family, the Lerneys. Sometimes in their grace they give thanks for their dead, including Peggie, and how our spirits soar when they do.

How we grievers long on the special days to have our loved ones acknowledged. Their absence. Their presence. To have others listen as we share our memories of them. To listen as others share their memories.

Well, that sad-glad sharing, too, is thanksgiving.

"I have Thanksgiving with number three son and his wife and her mother," says Gracie. "I'm welcome there, but I'm still alone, and when it's over there's no one to talk to about it.

"I talk to Al, but he doesn't answer me. I dream about him but never quite see him.

"And yet I'm thankful that everything that could be done for Al was done. I'm thankful that I had the crazy good sense not to put him on life support. I'm thankful that the doctor talked to me after Al died about the kind of man Al was."

Gracie's honoring the good even in Al's last hours sanctifies her Al's suffering, and her own.

"I'm thankful that Al had two years of retirement before he died. I'm thankful that when he was still working, he called me every noon. If I was out, I rushed to be home by then.

"At first all I remembered was what a great guy Al was, but later I remembered how we did battle, how he'd stalk me when I was under the hair dryer moving from room to room to get away from him. I buried *Saint Al* long ago, but I wouldn't change the life we had up and down and all around.

"Mostly I give thanks when I'm alone because the times I'm most thankful for are when Al and I were alone.

"It took a couple years for the memories to be happy, and even now they're not all happy. I *Cry Me a River* every Thanksgiving Day. *It's been six years, you big cry baby*, I tell myself, but I know how I feel. Thanksgiving helps me not to wish I'd never been born."

What is going to become of me now that . . . ?

One of the most common refrains we grievers wail—not sing but wail—is *What's going to become of me now that . . . ?* Well, one of the things I'm most thankful for since Joey and Peggie died is what has become of me.

When I asked Maryanne what good came to her from Mark's death, she yelled: "There are few people I'd take that question from, Meg. Yes, good has come to me since Mark's death and I'm grateful—I've learned to be authentic, for example—but you make it sound like I'm trading Mark for what I got.

"There's good in my life in spite of Mark's death. I smell the flowers, yes. I eat a good meal. But death is still in the air. You can't make me deny my pain. *I loved my son, Meg Woodson.*"

Whew! But, still, I admire your authenticity, Maryanne Janovich, and I quote you because many grievers respond to thoughts of good coming from their *love's* death with rage.

"I can't think of anything good that's come out of Al's death," says Gracie.

"Well, think again. Remember how the apostle Paul said, 'All things work together for good to them that love God'?"

"Yeah. Okay, I'm thinking. . . . Nope. Nothing."

But I know Gracie. I know good came to our church when she took Al's place on Consistory. I know she's become more self-reliant since Al's death, more reliant on God.

I'm not hinting, my fellow-griever, that you would have chosen that your *love* die for the good that has come to you. I maintain, however, that knowing you have not gone through *all that* for nothing can ease your pain as little else.

Not at first when you spend your hours on the rack screaming in pain. But soon.

We grievers long for transcendental meaning to our suffering, whether we know it or not. Bad things happen to all people, and we don't get far asking "Why?" Better to ask "How?" How can I use this bad thing for my good and the good of others?

Hear me, my grieving friend. You can give purpose to your pain. Giving purpose to your pain helps heal your pain.

I chose carefully to nurture and purposefully to expand my self-regard.

I'm not sure I would have survived my children's deaths as a functioning person had not their deaths pushed me into change.

I grew up pathologically shy. I was lonely all my life until my children came along, bonded with me, coveted my company.

And then my children *went away*.

After both of them had *gone*, I lay in bed one night clutching a bottle of Valium—ah, desolation—imagining how it would feel to empty the bottle into my mouth.

I knew I would not take the pills, fearing greater isolation, but how I fantasized—welcomed—the darkness that would come.

I *had to get help*, had to make a greater effort than any I had yet made to change.

Hallelujah—I changed.

Jan's mother was an alcoholic. Jan accepted responsibility for her mother's drinking and her father's happiness from her earliest days. When she married Craig, she assumed responsibility for his happiness without his assuming, or her assuming, any responsibility for her own.

"Only after Craig left," says Jan, "did I enter into a period of valuing myself. I had two choices. I could believe I deserved abandonment or I could never again enter into a relationship which did not add value to me. I chose carefully to nurture and purposefully to expand my self-regard."

Not all of us uncover such desperate need when we lose a *love*, but many of us do. We've had a taste of true love and cannot go back to false. Or perhaps the love we lost was sick love, made us sick, and we must now make ourselves well.

No, I would not have chosen that my children die for the good that has come to me, but they died, and I give thanks on Thanksgiving Day and every day for the good that has come.

To take it, to face it, to work through it, and eventually to convert it.

But the purpose we give to our pain can extend beyond ourselves. The verb *to comfort* means "to soothe" and "to strengthen." God is close to us in our pain, not only to soothe and strengthen us but to enable us to soothe and strengthen others.

"I've signed up for Hospice Training," says Jan. "I need something to put my healthy caring into. I'm well-versed in grieving. I'd like that experience to be an asset rather than a liability."

Being in counseling helped me so much after Peggie's death, I decided to go back to school and become a counselor. I was sure I'd never pass my MAT's. Never pass my first course. I'd always been a person who did well in school. Who would I be if I lost that identity?

Sometimes when something tough happens to us, the thing we must do to get through it is also tough.

Once I got into school, however, I loved the people, loved the learning. I needed something brand-new to give me a new start in life.

I don't think I knew back then all the reasons I chose counseling as a career, but I realize now that what I missed most about motherhood was feeding my children's minds and watching their spirits grow. One day I may write a book about the clients I see now in my small counseling practice—specializing in grief and depression and loneliness—and if I do, I'll call the book *Feeding Minds and Watching Spirits Grow.*

For his part, Joe became "grandfather" to a three-year-old girl in our church who needed a man in her life. We grievers are fortunate if the thing we do to fill the hole in us fills a hole in someone else as well.

"I pass a nursing home on my way to see you," says Sue. "An old man is always sitting outside in a wheelchair. I wave at him as I pass; I worry about him being alone out there. I wouldn't have looked twice at him before Suzette died. Does something bad have to happen to you before you care about others?"

You can bear the pain of your special days if you praise God in the midst of your pain.

You can bear the pain of your special days if you give purpose to your pain.

After his captivity in Lebanon, Terry Waite said:

> I have been determined in captivity, and still am deter-
> mined, to convert this experience into something that will
> be useful and good for other people. I think that's the way
> to approach suffering. It seems to me that Christianity
> doesn't in any way lessen suffering. What it does is enable
> you to take it, to face it, to work through it, and eventually
> to convert it.

I give thanks to God for loving me in all the days of my life.

I lived in the hospital for three weeks with Joey before
he died. On the second day, Joe shooed me out of Joey's
room and down to the cafeteria. I didn't want to leave my
son even to eat. How would I live without the notes he left
for me on the kitchen table when his father took him out?

Dear Mama,
    I have gone bowling with the Looney Ranger.
Hi-Ho Silver away.
    Sind,
    Your beloved son,
    Joseph Woodson, Jr.

Dear Mama,
    I have gone to the Hobby Shop with Tarzan. Oooh-
ooooh.
    Siend,
    Your beloved son,
    Joey W.

Where had a boy like Joey picked up a word like *beloved*, and why had he used it so consistently? Was it native to his being, the knowledge that he was my *beloved son*?

I sat in the cafeteria pushing a hamburger around on my plate, pulled a devotional book from my purse, and opened it at one particular page for no particular reason.

I remember nothing from the page but the heading at the top composed of words God had spoken from heaven two thousand years before to His Son, but which that night midst all the clatter of the cafeteria at Rainbow Babies and Children's Hospital, Cleveland, Ohio, He spoke to me: "You are my *beloved son*."

As though He were saying, "Do you love the boy lying so still upstairs between the white sheets? Do you want to be with him? Do you want to do things for him? Do you want to watch him grow into all he can become? Do you love him? Because if you do, you have some infinitesimal idea of how much I love you, my *beloved child*."

Even now I cannot record these moments-of-being-loved without weeping. Similar moments came again when I lived in the hospital with Peg while she was dying—moments of panic become moments of peace.

They heal me even now, as does knowing that people have read the books I've written about those times, some of whose lives have been lighted by my lighted moments.

Above all else I give thanks to God on Thanksgiving Day for loving me in all the days of my life, and, in some measure, for loving others through me. On Thanksgiving Day and every day I thank God for God.

Thank God.

Plan Ahead:

Place a horn of plenty on your Thanksgiving table. Ask family members to fill the horn with objects representing *the missing one*.

Fix mashed potatoes instead of sweet potatoes for your Thanksgiving meal. Have potluck. Eat out. Ask someone new to share your meal. Form a new family.*

Give thanks for three ways in which your *love* loved you best.

Give thanks for whatever *relief* you feel at your *love's* death or at your divorce.*

Give thanks for your ability to produce beauty out of the ashes of your life.*

---

* Indicates suggestions appropriate for those bereaved by divorce as well as death.

CHAPTER 9

Christmas

My heart is open wide tonight
  For stranger, kith or kin.
I would not bar a single door
  Where love might enter in.
                    Kate Douglas Wiggin

*W*hat is the toughest of the toughest days of the year for you?

My guess is Christmas. I say *guess* because we grievers are all different, and because the anniversary of the death of your *love* probably runs a close second.

Still, I pick Christmas as your toughest day.

Most of us grievers would just as soon be sick through the whole shebang!

I pick Christmas in part because it lasts so long.

A cartoon shows a woman walloping Santa Claus right out of his chair in the mall, with the caption: "Why don't you go back to the North Pole, buddy? It's not even Thanksgiving yet!"

Even if we limit our celebration of Christmas to its sacred aspect—hard to do if we turn on a TV or go to a store—it's still a celebration. The *season of joy* begins early and doesn't end till the end of New Year's Day.

"Christmas is about the birth of a baby, a baby who lived," says Ralph, twenty-two, his month-old baby dead of sudden infant death syndrome. "We're going to check into a motel on December 24 and not come out till Christmas is over."

"The best Christmas I've had since Al died," says Gracie, "is the one when I got the flu. I slept and slept, and when I woke up, Christmas was over."

Ralph and Gracie are talking about the day itself, but most of us grievers would just as soon be sick through the whole shebang!

"I tried to take my life after the holidays the year Ora died," says Jim. "Christmas is for families."

The second reason I pick Christmas as the toughest day of the year for grievers is that it emphasizes tradition, family tradition.

"You put the tree in the same spot you put it in last year," says Jan, "put the angel in the same spot on the tree—and you do it with the same people."

Yet if you're bereaved by death or divorce, nothing is the same—the friends gathered, the jokes told, the sense that your family will always be your family.

The biggest Christmas tradition of all is family reunion.

"It's the feeling of *home for Christmas* that gets to me," says Gracie, "cause all of a sudden there is no home as you know it. People invite you to their homes, but they don't serve the kind of food you fixed."

A third reason the holidays are *holocaust-days* for grievers is that they raise impossible expectations: Everyone will receive the gift coveted in their heart of hearts; decorations will be *Better Homes and Gardens* perfect; the stuffing will be moist. Adults will be gracious—all day long; children will be model children. We will all be as happy as we were as children. We will all be happier than we were as children.

Tinsel-draped, six-foot-tall, impossible expectations. On no other day do we count so much on things or events to make us happy.

If we are alone, on no other day do we feel so lonely. If we have no family to be with on Christmas Day, what does this say about us?

Here is the story of my first Christmas without Joey; and here, too, are my learnings from the story.

I began my first Christmas without Joey sitting at the top of the hall stairs with Peg. Early.

When the children were little, they roused the household at first light and led us in a shrieking, shoving charge down the stairs to the Santa Claus room. But as they grew older, and their parents older, they danced silently around their rooms first, hugging themselves and each other in anticipation of red-and-green-wrapped amazements to come.

And so I determined on Peg's first Christmas without her brother that I would be with her at that rising wonder hour, and we snuggled up against each other in our flannel nightgowns, she a young fourteen and I as old as pain.

I don't remember all we whispered about on the top step in that hushed house, but I wouldn't be surprised if we giggled over Joey and his Christmas walnut trick.

How the children loved walnuts. If you have cystic fibrosis, however, you can't digest nuts, so while we left a golden bowl of walnuts on the coffee table every Christmas, the rule was firm: one walnut a child a day.

"The thing I never figured out, Mother, was how Joey broke those walnuts open, ate the insides, and glued the shells back together so no one could tell.

"I mean, he knew he'd get caught in the end, but remember how he laughed at the shock on a person's face when they cracked open an empty nut? And how he'd act all innocent? He was so dumb, Mother."

I do remember talking to Peggie that morning about my Christmas dream. A book manuscript had been at a publisher for months. "Maybe an editor realized how I'd be feeling this Christmas, Peg, and mailed a contract special delivery yesterday so it would arrive today. If God were going to do something to get me through this Christmas, that would do it."

And then New York grandmother and grandfather, who had come to visit, pranced out of their room like high-stepping reindeer, as they always did, and Joe went downstairs first to light the Christmas tree, as he always did, and to position himself with his camera to catch Peg's first rays of rapture.

We'd always had two Christmas rooms: the living room—the true-meaning-of-Christmas room, and the family room—the Santa Claus room. The chimney was, after all, in the family room. This Christmas, however, we felt the need to change one *always* and switched the rooms about.

And, indeed, Peg gloried in excelsis in the living room that *first Christmas* morning over all the top items on her list: a clock radio, Probe, a French doll, religious jewelry, a Snoopy pencil sharpener, a Betsey Clark diary.

We went to the Holiday Inn for Christmas dinner. That, too, was tradition, grandmother and mother and daughter in their red dresses, mine a little tighter and Peg's a little shorter year by year. And after dinner we posed for a family picture in front of the big red sled in the lobby. Tradition.

As we drove home I caught myself thinking, *When is Joey going to get here and complete the Christmas picture?* . . . The Butterball turkey rolled like a bitter ball in my stomach.

I went to the cemetery that afternoon. Joe and my mother both offered to go with me, but I wanted *to be alone with Joey.*

As I parked in the cemetery, two men were rocking the car in front of me out of the snow—the only living souls beside me in that vast, frigid, tundra land.

I trudged from the road to Joey's grave in black boots, brown pants, black coat, wind whipping a green plaid scarf into my face. The day was dark and cold as ice, and I was an ice maiden.

As I bent low before Joey's grave, however, the frozen block that was my chest began to melt—and I wept.

Joseph Woodson, Jr.
Beloved Son and Brother

I wept for the mother and the father of this son. I wept for the sister of this brother. I wept for beloved Joey. "So brief a life, Joey. I miss you so."

And then I stood, fitted numb, gloved fingers into my pockets, pockets I'd stuffed with walnuts before leaving home. I tossed the walnuts on the small grave. "Merry Christmas, Joey. All the walnuts you want this year, Joey." I tossed the walnuts in profusion on my young son's grave.

And stumbled back to the car, its heater broken, engine clanging. "All our resources went into keeping you going, Joey. I tried my best to save you. Oh, Joey, I did try my best." Oh, how I wept. I wept myself out with sobs as bleak and violent as the day.

And by the time I got home, I felt much better.

The Toughest Days of Grief

But then I walked into the kitchen, blinded by its brightness, and there everyone sat around the table, warm and safe, hooting over a game of Parcheesi, and my tension mounted all over again.

No one mentioned Joey as the day wore on, and my tension continued to mount—and mount some more as Peggie used her new Snoopy pencil sharpener to sharpen twenty-four colored pencils, scattering multi-colored shavings throughout my Christmas-clean house.

When she would not cooperate for evening therapy, I exploded: "Joey never gave me this much trouble for therapy." I, who had never compared my children, out loud, in front of them, now compared my living child to my dead child.

Peg leaped off the therapy table and sprinted through the house yelling, "Father! Father, did you hear what Mother just said? She said Joey never gave her as much trouble as me! She compared me to Joey! Can you believe she did that?"

Everyone in the house knew of my perfidy. Everyone for several houses around knew.

Peg raced back to me. "I cannot believe you said that, Mother!"

But when finally I was permitted to go to bed that Christmas night, I found a typed note on my pillow, Peggie's forgiveness, the best of my presents: *Thou art the most wonderful mother in the whole world!!!*

The motto on the front of Peg's new Betsey Clark diary read: *Remembered Joys Are Never Past*.

Her first entry reads:

Dec. 26. "Remembered joys are never past." I shall prove this true in writing about Joey (among other things). I remember last year we had presents for Joey's teddy bear and friends. I made a yellow collar for Teddy and hat for Ms. Mildred, his wife. In Sears when we were buying a cube puzzle for Joey, I had to hide it under my hat to get it over to the counter without Joey seeing it.

I was just playing with Teddy. He was dancing to the music like he used to do with Joey.

It feels good to cry long and hard on Christmas Day.

We grievers think that on Christmas Day of all days we must not cry—must be merry. No. If there's one *must* for grievers on Christmas, it's this: We must cry, no guilt, no shame.

Reread chapter 3 for the value of tears when you're grieving and say to yourself: On no other day am I sad without my *love* as I'm sad without my *love* on Christmas Day.

You may be afraid you'll spoil Christmas for others if you cry. No, you'll snap others' heads off before Christmas is over if you don't. Better for others that you cry at some point through the day than spend the whole day artificially bright, or withdrawn, or pleading for pity.

It feels good to cry with others on Christmas Day.

I wish Peg and I had cried together on the top of the stairs on our first Christmas without Joey, but our family was emotionally closed with each other back then. And some of my grief was so much my own, I wanted to wrap my arms around myself as I cried. It would have been nice, though, as the day lingered, if someone else had wrapped their arms around me as I cried, too. I wish I had opened myself up to that.

Reread chapter 4. In what other season of the year are you so encouraged to make lists of what you want from others—to ask clearly for what you need?

Then, too, maybe your tears will trigger tears in others who need to have their tears triggered.

It feels good to get angry on Christmas Day.

Review the hand analogy in chapter 5: the soft underside of your hand your sadness, the hard top of your hand your anger—sadness and anger, different sides of the same emotion.

One reason it's hard not to get angry on Christmas is that you have so much to be sad-angry about. *Joey* isn't home for Christmas. *Joey* will never be home for Christmas again. Bang! Pow!

Why don't people leave you alone on Christmas? Why do people leave you alone? Why should you have to ask for what you need?

It's safer to get angry on Christmas than on other days because people who love you are more likely to forgive you then. I still have the note Peg wrote me on our *first Christmas*, misspelled "mots" and all.

It feels good to feel your guilt on Christmas Day.

Christmas brings out our perfectionism and our guilt for our lack of perfection as no other day. Back to impossible expectations.

Of course we should have done better for those we've lost. They're not here for Christmas, are they?

The unforgivable sin.

And how about the Christmas we got them something they didn't like and called them ungrateful because they didn't like it? *We did that on Christmas?*

If you feel guilty on Christmas Day, then it *feels good* to feel guilty consciously on Christmas Day. Reread chapter 6.

If you're guilt-prone, your sense of failure for not being the perfect Christmas person spreads back and forward over all your days.

Children of divorce are especially prone to guilt on Christmas. Which parent shall they spend Christmas with? How can they choose not to spend Christmas with either?

It feels good to feel—and feel away—your guilt on Christmas Day. It feels good to feel—and feel away—

your sadness and your loneliness and your anger on Christmas Day, too.

It feels good to feel merry as well as teary on Christmas Day.

Now, I'm not suggesting that you weep and rage and feel guilty all Christmas Day long. You may want to do most of your Christmas grief work a day or two before Christmas or early on Christmas morning so you can have merry moments through the day.

Yes, you may want to check into a motel and not come out till Christmas is over, forget all *old* Christmas habits. If that's what will best get you through the day, do that.

But don't close your mind to creating new rituals to spark your *young* Christmas joy. One couple I know went on a Caribbean cruise the Christmas after a drunk driver killed their daughter.

Or you may want to change just one or two traditions, like the room where you put the Christmas tree—fix things so the big difference isn't so stark.

Is putting up the tree or sending out cards more painful than helpful? Who else can do these things? What will happen if they don't get done? You don't have your usual energy; if you exhaust yourself physically, you'll deplete your emotional reserves just when you need them most.

Decide ahead of time what Christmas parties you will pass by this year, and build supports ahead of time for those you will join in. Prepare your hostess for your early departure. Order the gifts you bring from a catalog.

Your worst Christmas may not be your first Christmas. You may numb your way through your first Christmas, so don't be surprised if the pain hits you harder in later years.

Be thoughtful of yourself on all the Christmases of your grief.

Christmas Day is a good day to practice feeling good. Reread chapter 2 for the benefits of setting up happy times for yourself.

It feels good to give thanks on Christmas Day.

How we grievers fear all along our way that our dead will be forgotten, that their lives will cease to have meaning for others.

Joe and I will create a Remembrance-Thanksgiving Centerpiece for our dining room table this Christmas with a wise man in the middle that Joey made in the third grade out of a toilet paper roll; surrounded by a variety of sequined ornaments that Peg made for her friends each Christmas; with a needle and thread standing guard at the edge of the circle in memory of my seamstress mother, a screwdriver and screws for my handyman father, a receipt from the May Co. in memory of the shopping sprees Joe's mother took us on.

No, we won't foist an explanation of our centerpiece on others, but it will be there to help if others want to help us thank God on Christmas Day for what our *loves* meant to

The Toughest Days of Grief

us, or to thank God for what our *loves* meant to them. Re-read chapter 8.

Talking about our *loves* on Christmas is a way we grievers have of bringing them *home for Christmas.*

It feels good to give purpose to your pain on Christmas Day.

Joe and I will put a poinsettia in church this Christmas, let its bright red reflection of the gladness of our children's lives gladden the lives of our church family. And we'll make a donation to the Cystic Fibrosis Foundation, too, in hope that children with C.F. in our world family will celebrate more Christmases than did our children.

Perhaps you'll want to invite each member of your family to choose one of their prized possessions, wrap it, and give it to someone in need. Or you may want to pick a neighbor who's out of a job and leave a box of foodstuffs at his door, quiet as a Christmas mouse.

That last suggestion calls back Christmases of my childhood when my father was out of work and our church brought baskets of canned goods, each can wrapped in white tissue paper, to our house on Christmas Eve.

I puzzled over why my mother cried at such a marvel. I tore the paper off those cans in a frenzy of glee. I didn't cry—till now.

Most of us grievers have a history of loss in addition to our current loss. We know what it's like *to be without.* Who is better prepared for a season of giving than we? Of all people, we grievers know what it means to have someone touch our pain with their love.

It feels good on Christmas Day, and on New Year's Day, to look at what lies ahead for your love.

One thing we grievers grieve for on Christmas Day is that our *love* is missing Christmas. One thing we grieve for on New Year's Day is that our *love* has no new year ahead. No new dreams for him, or so we think. No new growth to strive for.

And so it feels good to incorporate Easter (chapter 11) into Christmas and New Year's (chapter 10), to recognize that our *love* has found that elusive, perfect Christmas, that our *love* is living in endless celebration of new life ahead.

When Peggie was in the seventh grade, she made a list she titled: *What I Know I'm Going to Like about Heaven.*

1. Everyone will like me and be nice to me.
2. I will like everybody and be nice to them.
3. I will be able to run and not get tired.
4. Everyone will get highest honors, and everybody will be happy for everybody else—no competition.
5. I will be noticed by God.
6. I will have more friends than most people in heaven waiting for me (all the C.F. kids who died).

7. When I meet God, it will not be a gloomy day with storms and thunder and this chariot and all these horses coming to punish bad people like Mrs. Drummond said in Sunday school. (She made me so mad making categorical statements about something she knows nothing about.)

8. Although I still see this stupid picture when I think of heaven of clouds and an angel with a harp hanging up stars, heaven will not be like that. Actually, it will be better than anything I could imagine, so there is no use in trying to figure it out.

9. A rose will still be a rose in heaven, it will just smell ten times sweeter. (I heard a preacher say that.)

Yes.

I would not bring my children back from their Easter world if I could, but one day I will go to them. Reunion.

Not that they would rush us, but how our merry dead must long for us to be merry.

It feels good to notice God noticing you on Christmas Day.

God gave His Child to us as a gift on the very first Christmas because we are His *loves*. Nothing feels as good when we're bereaved of love as breathing in new love. Reread chapter 7.

God *coming to me* is what Christmas is about for me since my children went away from me—to Him.

You can get through the pain of all your special days.

I put this chapter on Christmas toward the end of this book so I could use it for review. Christmas calls forth and intensifies all the feelings called forth by all our special days, yet on no other day—unless we stop ourselves—do we feel so obligated to get through our feelings without feeling them.

Stop yourself.

You can get through the pain even of Christmas Day.

Plan Ahead:

Count on having an imperfect Christmas.*

Hang up a stocking for your *love* on Christmas Eve and suggest that family members leave notes for *her* in the stocking.

Spend a few minutes acting *as if* you are merry on Christmas Day. Shoulders back. Head high. Lips smiling. Eyes sparkling.*

Encourage a family cry on Christmas Day.*

Place a Christmas wreath on your *love's* grave, and on an unremembered grave of someone unknown to you.

---

* Indicates suggestions appropriate for those bereaved by divorce as well as death.

CHAPTER 10

· ·

New Year's

· ·

What we call the beginning is often the end.
And to make an end is to make a beginning.
The end is where we start from.

T. S. Eliot

· ·

*W*e grievers are an insecure lot, *abandoned* as we've been, but never do we worry as we worry on New Year's Day: that we won't be able to go on; that our pain will go on; that we'll know more losses—that we plain won't make it through the year's long night.

We didn't welcome the holidays when they came, yet how woebegone we feel as we head back into everydayness.

Life's basic truth bears down on us: all love comes with impermanence built in. Oh, yes. And no miracle arrives by mail to take the pain away.

And what are we left with but fear? Fear of yet another round of three hundred and sixty-five days.

***Use New Year's Day to take the strangeness, the offense,
out of your pain.***

I'm embarrassed to admit that I once hoped for a book
contract on Christmas Day.

"My goodness, Mother," Peg said as we sat on the top
of the stairs, "with such ridiculous expectations, no wonder you get depressed."

But we grievers can work at inner miracles: work hard
at growing up enough to accept life as it is; work hard and
long at growing strong enough to master life as it is.

No, your pain isn't going to go away anytime soon, and,
yes, you probably will know more losses before your life is
over. So? Life is like that. Oh, yes.

I'm not suggesting that you take the pain out of your
pain, only that you use New Year's Day to take the
strangeness, the offense, out of your pain.

"Aren't all these notes," wrote C. S. Lewis after the
death of his wife, "the senseless writhings of a man who
won't accept the fact that there is nothing we can do with
suffering except to suffer it? Who still thinks there is some
device (if only he could find it) which will make pain not
to be pain."

***We grievers know what grief is, and we know that we
must do it.***

Some of the worst pain grievers tell me about comes
from friends and family members who avoid them because

of their loss. Such people keep from acknowledging the pain in their own lives by avoiding pain in the lives of others, and by their full-tilt pursuit of pleasure. Our grief shakes the foundation of their pleasure-is-my-right world.

"I was always close to my cousin," Elaine, a new widow, weeps in my office. "She was the only family besides my husband I had, and she often told me I was the only family she had. But when Adam died, she found excuse after excuse to pull away from me.

"Last week I arranged to visit her on Thursday afternoon at two o'clock, but when I arrived at her house, she wasn't there—sauntered in an hour later. 'I hope you didn't mind waiting,' she said. 'There were long lines in the supermarket.'

"And then in a rare touch of honesty, she added, 'You talk about Adam's death all the time, you know. It's hard for me to handle.'

"'But I know it's hard for you to handle. That's why I don't talk to you about it at all.'

"'Well, maybe not,' she said, 'but it seems like you do . . . His death happened to you, didn't it?'"

It's not unusual for relatives to send the message in what seems grievous irony to grievers: *You lost your family. Stay away from mine.*

Another client tells me that every time he goes to church, fellow members treat the death of his wife as a spiritual defeat.

"Sunday after Sunday," he says, "their disappointed, disapproving eyes look *lovingly* into mine. *Poor thing*, those eyes say. *You didn't have enough faith, did you?*

"*You did it, you killed your wife,* those eyes say, and never see the horror shoot through mine when they say it.

"'So are you over it yet?' they ask Sunday after Sunday, wanting me *over it* not for my sake but for their peace of mind."

How they hurt us, these blood families and church families, who will not let our grief be grief

But we grievers know what grief is and we know that we must *do it*, especially as we stand in the doorway to a new year and look down the road at all the pure white *can't lie* days on which nothing has yet been written. Better to be in touch with reality, however frightful, than to renounce reality.

Lucky us. We grievers know that we will scribble many days of the innocent new-born year black with our grief. We know that we will heal. But not quickly. And not easily. And never totally.

Use only those resolutions that will quiet your terror — that will open your heart to the future.

As I look back through this book, my fellow grievers, I worry at the number of injunctions I've given you. Take a vacation. Cry. Don't isolate yourself. Get mad. Feel your guilt . . . And now I'm urging New Year's resolutions upon you.

Please, ignore any suggestions that overwhelm you. Make only those resolutions that will quiet your terror— that will open your heart to the future.

Yes, on-going grief is okay, but so is *going on* beyond grief.

Resolution: I will put a God Box on my refrigerator. I will not let my fears for the new year buzz half-formed around my head but will give each one a swat and capture it in my God Box.

I will not face my fears for the New Year alone in the cosmos. I will not face my fears alone in my one-bedroom apartment.

Resolution: I will create a best possible new year fantasy. Detailed. Long. I will share my fantasy with another. Create images. Expand my fantasy every morning:

I will fashion a bedroom all my own—my dream room. The curtains will drift like pale mauve fairy hair from ceiling to floor. I will replace the king-size bed with a twin bed, the mattress so soft it will cuddle me each night into peaceful sleep. The downy spread will be of deepest mauve with violets and lilacs sprouting across it, and the sheets and pillowcases and even the skirt on my dressing table will match.

Where *Bob's* dresser once stood, I will put a sewing machine and sewing cabinet of mellow oak. I will reorganize my patterns, stock the thread drawer. I will make myself violet lounging pajamas to wear as I work loungingly in my very own sewing nook.

Resolution: I will write statements of affirmation about myself:

—I was created to create.

—I want change and I can bring about change.

—I am learning to be both responsible and playful.

—I choose to be physically healthy this New Year.

—I will make two new friends.

Repeat your affirmations ten times every day. Act out one of your resolutions every day—your resolutions, not mine.

The air of confidence you put into your subconscious mind reduces your conscious anxiety. Intentionality can be a form of prayer. Make prayer a form of intentionality.

Remembered joys are never past.

The second entry in Peg's *A Remembered Joy Is Never Past* diary reads:

Jan. 1 Last year on New Year's Eve Joey and I went into mother's and father's room at midnight with pots and pans and spoons to bang on them. Father put his head under the covers and just kept groaning over and over, "Go away. Go away."

Then we all had hot chocolate out of a thermos. It had been made up ahead of time.

Don't confuse letting go of your grief with letting go of your *love*. Remembered joys *are* never past. Joe and I *had* those bang-up midnight moments with our children. Joe and I *have* those moments.

We grievers are prone to feel that only our grief ties us to our *love*. No. The movement of grief is away from sad memories to happy memories. As your pain over the absence of your *love* decreases, your joy in the presence of your *love* increases. Yes.

Carlotta says, "I carry Suzette with me in my heart."

Oh, yes.

Still, I vow every year that this year I will not *do the holidays*, that I will close my eyes to Christmas stars, my ears to New Year's bells.

But every year I *do the holidays* for Joe's sake. And every year it's tough. I know you know, my grieving friend, how tough. But every year we get through the holidays, don't we? I tell you, if we grievers can get through Christmas Day and New Year's Day, we can get through every day.

And so for the New Year, my grieving friend, for all your brand-new years, I wish for you the great courage to hurt and, in your time, the greater courage to heal.

Oh, yes. Yes.

Choose life.

Plan Ahead:

Have a candlelighting ceremony on New Year's Eve: a blue candle for past joys, a red candle for present courage, a yellow candle for hope for the future.*

Toast five *constants* in your life.*

At New Year's dinner give a wallet-size folder of snapshots of your *love* to each person present.

Write three sentences about the New Year in which you use the word *new* in an exciting way.*

Memorize the promises of God concerning His presence in all your new years:*

> I will never leave you nor forsake you.
>
> I will be with you always, even unto the end of the world.

---

* Indicates suggestions appropriate for those bereaved by divorce as well as death.

CHAPTER 11

Easter

Though they go mad they shall be sane,
Though they sink through the sea they shall
    rise again
Though lovers be lost love shall not;
And death shall have no dominion.

                                    Dylan Thomas

April is the cruellest month, breeding
Lilacs out of the dead land.

                                    T. S. Eliot

*E*aster means yellow tulips ... scent of lilacs ... warm breezes. Easter means hope. Hope supposedly springs eternal in the spring—but not for grievers. Not at first.

April is the cruelest month....

No, for grievers spring often means springtime depression. Counselors see more depressed people in the springtime than at Christmastime.

We don't want to take off our woolen coats, fur-lined gloves, the coverings with which we've insulated our bodies and our woes. But the frozen months pass, the unwrapping comes—we stand exposed—and all our fancies turn to thoughts of love lost. We have no choice but to thaw, and the thawing hurts too much.

How do we handle cherry blossoms when, in contrast to earth's happiness, our unhappiness feels unhappier still?

I present springtime depression as a prologue to Easter, a kind of *Good Friday One*, so at least you'll know what's happening if you're down in this triumphant season.

> *April is the cruellest month, breeding*
> *Lilacs out of the dead land.*

My God, My God, why have you forsaken me?

The *absence of God* rocked my soul after Joey died, creating for me a *Good Friday Two*.

For several years before Joey died, I went to Eucharist on Saturday afternoons. St. Bartholomew was my trysting place and that hour was my time to be Held, to be Loved. How needily I went back to St. Bart's after Joey's death—but God did not come. Week after week, God did not come. *What was He thinking?*

Nobody talked in church about God *not* being there at their point of need. I felt singled out by His absence.

But then here and there I came upon people who admitted that in their grief, they, too, wandered in ultimate shades. C. S. Lewis, for example, in his book *A Grief Observed*, wrote of his experience after the death of his wife:

> Meanwhile, where is God? . . . go to Him when your need is desperate, when all other help is vain, and what do you find? A door slammed in your face, and a sound of bolting and double bolting on the inside. After that, silence. . . . There are no lights in the windows. . . . It might be an empty house. Was it ever inhabited? . . .
>
> Of course it's easy enough to say that God seems absent at our greatest need because He *is* absent—non-existent. But then why does He seem so present when, to put it quite frankly, we don't ask for Him?

But then later in the book, Lewis wrote of a day when he was less exhausted than he had been, his heart lighter:

> And so . . . I have gradually been coming to feel that the door is no longer shut and bolted. . . . The time when there is nothing at all in your soul except a cry for help may be just the time when God can't give it: you are like the drowning man who can't be helped because he clutches and grabs. Perhaps your own reiterated cries deafen you to the voice you hoped to hear.
>
> On the other hand, "Knock and it shall be opened." But does the knocking mean hammering and kicking the door like a maniac? . . . After all, you must have a capacity to receive, or even omnipotence can't give.

Six months after Joey's death, I, too, found that the Light once more glowed in the windows of my *habitation*.

I was never unaware of God's presence after Peggie died, perhaps because the second death, while *a second death*, was not as crushing of my confidence in God or in myself as the first.

Joe says, "My awareness of God's presence after the children's deaths was no more or less than it's always been." Joe is not as inward-looking or questioning as I.

Now not for a moment do I believe that God was not with me when I could not feel Him with me. Did He ever not forsake Christ more than when Christ cried, "My God, My God, why have you forsaken me?"

Wait, my fellow-griever. Bear your way through your Good Friday with what confidence you can muster that Easter will come. It will come whether you have confidence that it will or not. It is not in the nature of God to desert you in a time of need. He cannot do that.

We are their loves as surely as they are ours.

For many of us grievers, a *Good Friday Three* grows out of our disappointment that our *loves* have not *come back* to us.

I'm not talking about conjuring up our dead in seances, but about the kind of experience Norman Vincent Peale had when he felt his mother's hand on his forehead after her death; and when, as he stood before a group of ministers, he saw his long-dead minister-father walk up the aisle—not the old man who had died, but a man bursting with the prime of life.

People who have these experiences talk about having them, while people who don't have them don't talk about not having them, so it appears to lonely, longing grievers that more people *see* their dead or *feel a hand on their head* than do.

Grief experts say: Some people have these psychic experiences and some people don't. No one knows why.

Still, we wouldn't feel so bad about our dead not coming back if other people's dead didn't.

Perhaps some people are more open to these experiences. Perhaps some people need them more. Perhaps God gives them to some people, like Norman Vincent Peale, so they can use them to reassure others.

Neither Joe nor I have had any sense of our children's presence since their deaths. If we had, would once have been enough, or would we still be waiting for their next coming in a way that impeded our acceptance of their final going?

How long would we be sure that our *touch* had not come out of our aching subconscious? And do we want to call our children back from blissful heaven to bleary earth?

The images of my children I hold in my flesh and blood mind are of them in their flesh and blood: Peg sitting next to me on the couch each Christmas as we watched *The Nutcracker*, Peg in her leaden body thrilling to those lithesome bodies leaping high, drinking in the beauty her soul was parched for, looking up at me with tears pouring down her cheeks. "Oh, Mother—she had to go back—to the playroom—and she lost—her prince."

Joey, the stunted-growth boy, holding up his minuscule wrist: "How come, Mom, the other boys in my class have wrists that are big around and my wrist is only this-big around?"

Joey, the magician, claiming my attention with cape and potions.

And, as always, Joey, the love-note writer. What love, what joy he brought me. "You are the joy of my life, Joey," I told him again and again.

I didn't often let him see me cry, but once when I did, he went into my study and then came out and threw a torn-off piece of paper at me on which he had scrawled:

Dear Mama,
    You are the joye to my life.
Siened,
Your Beloved Son

I'm sure of two things: (1) that our dead do not come back to us because they do not love us. We are their *loves* as surely as they are ours; or more surely, since they love now more purely than we. And (2) that if we do not know in our hearts that our dead love us, one more evidence will not convince us.

It wasn't proof of my children's love I wanted when I looked for signs of their presence. I wanted my children back.

But we grievers can't have our dead back; that is why we're grievers.

Don't let the yellow cellophane of Easter keep you from your shroud feelings.

In *A Letter of Consolation*, Henri J. M. Nouwen writes to his father about their first Easter without mother and wife:

> We both shall remember how she loved this great feast, how she decorated . . . the dinner table with purple and yellow ribbons. Somehow it seems long, long ago. . . . Her death changed our experience of time. . . . Every "normal" experience . . . has the quality of a "first time." . . . The First Christmas without mother, the first New Year without mother. . . . Easter was not only an important day to celebrate, but a day to celebrate with her . . . so much so that we could not distinguish between the joys brought to us by the feast and the joys brought to us by her presence at the feast.

Each time we face one of the three *great holidays* of the year—Easter, Thanksgiving, Christmas—our *love* comes alive in us again—and dies in us again.

These family-oriented holidays touch our human core. These church holidays touch our spiritual core. How can we grievers bear these happiest, holiest days of the year?

We turn to our grief not only on Good Friday but on Resurrection Sunday as well. As nature's new life heightens our *deadness* in the spring, so does the new life and the family life of Easter.

We mustn't let the yellow cellophane of Easter keep us from our shroud feelings.

Easter may be the time to crack the stone that blocks the exit.

But neither must we let our shroud feelings keep us from the true meaning of Easter: namely, that our dead are not in their sepulchers, and that sooner or later it will be time for us grievers to come forth from ours.

I've rattled the stones sealing our tombs on Good Friday so those of us who have grieved our three days will be able to come forth on Easter Sunday.

Some of us emerge from our tombs so gradually we're not aware that we're doing it. We blink in the rosy morning light, gulp in the fresh air, and go our blessed way. Others have to make a conscious effort to get out. And still others don't want to get out. We are used to being sad, and even if we have not used our sadness as an attention-getting device, it has been that. Who will we be if we're not sad and needy? Will anyone hold us close?

The biggest reason, however, that we hold on to our grief is that it connects us to our dead. Our sad memories are all we have left of them, or so we think, and we clutch the sadness with our own death grip lest we have nothing left of them at all.

If you have to make an all-out effort to unclutch your *love*, Easter time may be your time. Of course this may be your first Easter without husband . . . or sister or grandmother. You may have time yet to serve in your tomb. But even so Easter may be the time to crack the stone that blocks your exit, to take a stab at happiness, lest the time comes when you have nothing left of it at all.

Here are a few things we can do to let a beam of Easter light break in upon us.

• Become aware of joy that's crept—unawares—back into our lives. We're so used to thinking of ourselves as nothing-but-sad that we need to step back from time to time and say, "Hey, I don't feel that sad all the time anymore."

• Concentrate on the fact that while we don't have our *loves* anymore, we did have them. Our habit is to say, "I miss the way my son bounded in from school each day." But as time passes we can change that to, "I smile remembering the way my son bounded in from school each day."

Do you recognize this as an ongoing theme in this book?

Our sad memories need not be all we have left. Happy memories are so much better.

• Recognize the joy in which our *loves* are now living. I had to make a deliberate effort to do this, and I made it at Easter time.

Spring is never spring for me unless I find a dogwood tree to look up into. It's not enough for me to look at a dogwood. I must find one whose branches bend low, stand underneath it, and gaze upward—encompassing myself with the mass of blossoms.

The spring I decided to *let* my children enter eternal spring, I created a fantasy that took place on such a spot. . . .

I stood gazing up into a dogwood tree when, before my eyes, the trunk of the tree grew upward and the branches grew downward. Up, up, and down, till I found myself rooted in a living cathedral, maybe a hundred feet in circumference, the branches meeting overhead in a domed ceiling a hundred feet high.

The branches singing low in a higher-world ensemble of strings—violins and harps perhaps—with the fluting of some untamed wild-wind instrument—or was it birdsong—sounding hope and joy through the melody of . . . a cradle song?

No . . . a bridal hymn. Someone or someones were *plighting their troth* to me *till death did us not part.*

God, I thought. God is in this place. God—and my children—are in this place loving me.

I stumbled to one edge of the living tabernacle, blinded by the purity of a million white blooms, hands shielding my ears from perfection of sound, and sank to the grass, my back to the wall of flowers.

And when finally I could take the beauty in, be made beautiful myself within by it, the light filtering through the bower became brighter still as a small figure walked through the wall of flowers opposite me.

No, oh, no! But could it be? *Dear God—Joey.*

He walked to the middle of *the sacred place* and stopped. "Hi, Mom." He *thought* the words to me. And I *thought* back, "Hi, Joey." And he laughed the way he'd always laughed, one foot kicking high, both arms flailing, and though I only *heard* him in my mind, it was the biggest boy-laugh I'd ever heard.

And I threw back my head and laughed with him—I couldn't believe I was sitting there matter-of-factly laughing with Joey—not because anything was funny but because everything was full of delight.

He was still thin, but wiry rather than sick-thin, and he stretched one arm out of his Cleveland Indians jacket to show me how big around his wrist was.

I knew that if I looked at that moment into the chest where I kept mementoes of my children, the Cleveland Indians jacket would be there along with the tennis shoes with the red stars and the jeans he was wearing.

He looked like he'd grown younger. I couldn't stop staring. Or maybe it was more innocent, though he'd always been *my innocent.* I'd never thought of holiness as looking young, but maybe that's what holiness was—unspoiled, innocent happiness.

I cried for a minute because Joey's wrist was *just like the other boys*, but I knew that my tears sparkled with joy.

A part of me ached to tell my son how sorry I was I'd said, *Bring Joey Home*. But I was still his mother; I knew my son had forgiven me for everything that needed forgiving. And more to the point, I knew that Joey *was home*, and glad to be there, thank you very much.

And then Joey, the magician, pulled a scrap of paper from his pocket, which, as he flourished it high, became a scroll that reached to the ground. Then with another *ta-ta* he took a magic marker—red, his favorite color—out of his other pocket and wrote on the scroll:

Dear Mama
   I have gone to heaven with Jesus.
Signd,
Your beloved son,
Joseph Woodson, Jr.

And then he just looked at me, hopping up and down, and the love that flowed out of him toward me stopped my breathing, and I looked away.

And when I looked back, he had stepped to one side, and Peg walked through the dogwood. And my heart stopped again, but I did not turn away.

Peggie looked *older*. I use the word for lack of a better one. She wore the navy cords and the navy blue T-shirt with the 23 on the front—both in the cedar chest—she'd worn on her twenty-third birthday and again during her final hospitalization, and navy blue socks, no shoes.

I hadn't known that not-hurting-physically anymore, or that not not-being-loved-enough anymore would make a person look *older*, but there was a settledness about her, a radiant calm, as though at last she'd got to where she'd always wanted to be.

For a moment I thought, *She's beyond where I am. I've lost her.* And the pain shot through me.

But then she *said*, "Hi, Ma," the way she'd always called me *Ma* to cover deep feeling, and I felt the same unspeakable love flow from her I'd felt from Joey. Felt like I'd died and gone to heaven . . .

And then the music changed subtly, teased my brain with the familiar, yet not familiar. And then my cystic-fibrosis daughter, my Margaret Ann Woodson of the *leaden body*—danced. The Nutcracker, of course, or something close to it. Oh, how she leaped and twirled and pirouetted. On and on. Round and round our enchanted meeting place, higher and higher.

And when I thought I could bear no more, as the dance slowed to an end, Peg flashed two thoughts to me. "She doesn't have to go back to the playroom, Ma." And, "She found her prince."

I threw my head back and sobbed—in front of my children. Sobbed away doubt I hadn't known was there. Sobbed away fear—for them, for me—fear of what I did not know. Sobbed away the rusty stain of my grief and its power to corrode my soul. I sobbed my soul inside out. And then I stopped.

And Peg and Joey stood, together now, hands joined, and bowed to me, honored me—my tears, my end of tears, I didn't know what—in a way they had never honored me on earth, and were gone. In a blink. And the bower was gone.

Too soon. All gone. I thought I must die if it were gone. I shut my eyes and made believe it was not gone, but I knew it was gone because my back hurt from leaning against the prickly trunk of that puny dogwood tree, and ants crawled up my pants.

I sat forever, it seemed, adjusting to my *spoiled* world— How could I live here?—but in time letting my new world cast its spell over the old.

We love you still, Mother. No criticism, no disappointment in their tones.

You're alive to us still, Mother. As though we had not been apart. As though they had not . . . forgotten me.

But, oh, Mother, don't wait for us to come to you. We're waiting for you, Mother, to come to us.

> *Strange how life is rounded*
> *By darkness become light.*
> —*Murray Bodo*

To forgive my children for dying, to bless them on their way and myself on my way without them.

I went into the hospital recently for surgery. I waited for hours on a hard bed for my time. The surgery required general anesthesia, and for some time my heart had been acting funny. I didn't want it to stop.

The Toughest Days of Grief

But, then, I spent my waiting time reading life-after-life stories, and by the time they wheeled me away, I almost hoped it would.

I'm comfortable with my springtime fantasy because it reflects the experiences of the near-dead or newly-dead in the many life-after-life books I've read now. They pull you into life-more-real: greener grass, brighter light, the greater beauty of flowers, music "like the speech of angels," the ease of movement, the instant *knowing* of another.

Surely my fantasy does not do justice to the next life, but neither, I think, does it do it violence.

Once when Peg had been at the point of death, she told me that a cameo "just fell into my head, Mother, like a cameo in an old-fashioned fairy tale book, only smudged around the edges. A cameo of sunshine and butterflies and meadow flowers."

After Suzette died, the people who loved her saw butterflies everywhere. At first I thought, *Ah, wishful thinking that they have to do with Suzette. It must be a year for butterflies.*

But then on Easter Sunday, little Carlotta—Suzette's best friend—sat with her father on their front steps and said, "I'm going to take care of Suzette's little sister now. I'm going to do it for Suzette." And two big yellow butterflies flew in front of her face.

And soon after Easter, Sue ran the Revco Marathon. She ran it *for Suzette.* The day was hot and humid, and she finished hours later than expected, but when she got home, her sister called from Nebraska. "Did you finish the marathon at 2:20?"

"That's exactly when I finished."

"I knew it. Two big yellow butterflies flew in front of my face at 2:20."

I encourage you, my fellow-griever, to create a fantasia-feeling for where your *love* is. Remember what diminished him or her in this world and remove that hindrance from the next. Remember what he or she only dreamed of in this world and incorporate the fulfillment of those dreams in your dream. Lure yourself into "an echo of the invisible world."

One of the things that kept Sue from *letting go* of Suzette was her fear that no one was taking care of her. "Do you think Peggie's watching after Suzette, Meg?"

"Maybe. Peg loved taking care of little children."

Still, Sue's fear persisted, till Easter, her first without Suzette, the Easter of the butterflies, when it came to Sue on a brilliant flutter of truth, *Suzette's okay. God's got her.*

One of the things that's kept me from *letting go* of Peg and Joey is their not having had a chance to leave more of their mark on this earth. I'd poured so much into them— for what? But they seemed so comfortable with me in my *vision*, and they knew what I needed from them. Who's to say they're not leaving more of their mark on earth from heaven than they could have from earth?

Of course, the moon madness still settles upon me at times, the epic sorrow.

So I train myself to *have Easter* many times throughout the seasons of the year—to *forgive* my children for dying, to bless them on their way, and myself On My Way Without Them.

They are, after all, with the One who comes to me in the Eucharist, and it is that glimpse, not fantasized, into how they are being loved and Who is loving them that loosens my grip on them.

They are with the resurrected Christ, who came out of His tomb on Easter, and He is with me. Can they be far away?

In his book *The Song of the Sparrow*, Murray Bodo says:

> On clear days . . . when the wind blows all day long, everything seems cleaner somehow, and it is easy to puff up your lungs and inhale spring. There are soul days like that, too. Something clicks inside and everything seems bright and clear again. . . . and it is easy to praise God for all the lightness you feel within. It is spring in your soul.

Several years after Peggie's death, John O'Byrne, Peg's best friend, said:

> The experience of Peggie's death was an affirmation of my faith. It happened and I survived it. It brought me closer to God. I can't explain it. I'm not afraid of my own death now, and I'm not as afraid of the deaths of the people I care about.
>
> I have a total belief that Peggie went to a better place— an innate understanding that this has taken place.

I have a new sensitivity to the *gift* of life. There was never a time I forgot Peg wasn't alive, but the message of her death was: *Get on with* your *life*. As awful as her death was, it left me feeling incredibly alive.

Rise up.

I wish for you all—my fellow-grievers all—that in your time and in your way you will *rise up*.

Plan Ahead:

Write an Easter note from your *love* to you. What does *he* want you to know? To feel?

Take a blanket and a thermos of coffee, climb a hill on Easter morning, and watch the sun rise.*

Stand in your favorite outdoor spot and *decide* to trust the growth process—in nature, and in you.*

Fantasize reunion with your *love*. A never-has-to-end bear hug? What?

Have a tree-planting ceremony in memory of your *love* in which friends and family members mention the qualities of your *love* that live on in them.

---

* Indicates suggestions appropriate for those bereaved by divorce as well as death.

The Toughest Days of Grief